YES, YOU CAN GET
A FINANCIAL LIFE!

YES, YOU CAN GET A FINANCIAL LIFE!

YOUR LIFETIME GUIDE TO FINANCIAL PLANNING

BEN STEIN AND PHIL DeMUTH

NBP

NEW BEGINNINGS PRESS
Carlsbad, California

Published by: New Beginnings Press, Carlsbad, California

Distributed in the United States by: Hay House, Inc.: www.hayhouse.com • *Distributed in Australia by:* Hay House Australia Pty. Ltd.: www.hayhouse.com.au • *Distributed in the United Kingdom by:* Hay House UK, Ltd.: www.hayhouse.co.uk • *Distributed in the Republic of South Africa by:* Hay House SA (Pty), Ltd.: orders@psdprom.co.za • *Distributed in Canada by:* Raincoast: www.raincoast.com • *Distributed in India by:* Hay House Publications (India) Pvt. Ltd.: www.hayhouseindia.co.in

Editorial supervision: Jill Kramer • *Design:* Tricia Breidenthal

Library of Congress Cataloging-in-Publication Data

Stein, Benjamin.
  Yes, you can get a financial life! : your lifetime guide to financial planning / Ben Stein and Phil DeMuth.
     p. cm.
  Includes bibliographical references and index.
  ISBN-13: 978-1-4019-1124-9 (hardcover : alk. paper)
  ISBN-13: 978-1-4019-1125-6 (tradepaper : alk. paper) 1. Finance, Personal--United States. 2. Investments--United States. 3. Financial security--United States. I. DeMuth, Phil, 1950- II. Title.

HG179S55858 2007
332.02400973--dc22   2006020272

Hardcover ISBN: 978-1-4019-1124-9
Tradepaper ISBN: 978-1-4019-1125-6

10 09 08 07   4 3 2 1
1st edition, February 2007

Printed in the United States of America

FOR RACHEL, STEPHANIE,
AND CHRISTOPHER

CONTENTS

CHAPTER 1

PERSONAL FINANCE OVER THE LIFE CYCLE

Life is short. Life is precious.

It's far too short and precious to lie awake worrying about money at three o'clock in the morning. Your authors have done so, and take it from us—it isn't worth it. Even the most blameless lives can be ruined by wondering where the money will come from to pay for a set of braces. The most charming guy or gal with good manners and nice teeth can be cast down into a pit of anxiety and self-loathing by wondering how to finance a child's first year at Amherst College ($50,000 and rising as of 2006).

Men and women who are kind to their children, loving to their dogs and cats, and unselfish with their time when friends are getting divorced still find that their peace of mind—one of the few really meaningful assets in this world—can be snatched away when a credit card is rejected. When perfectly fine people look back upon the last ten years of their lives, that decade can seem as if it were a blur of falling leaves, gray afternoons before a fireplace, and crowded trains and freeways, but then—like a horrible scar cutting across it all—there were the nights spent worrying about where the funds to pay for it all would come from.

That need not happen, of course, and that's what this book is about. Life should be for love and work, not worrying about money. Everyone will experience totally unexpected financial crises that no amount of preparation could have prevented, and there will probably be some windfalls, too. The nature of life is to be unpredictable in all its small details (and even in its large ones). We can't control every event.

Those nights of lying in bed and hearing the neighbor's dog bark while you wonder how you'll tell your wife that her mother will have to move out of the good private nursing home into some miserable public one—and indeed, most other bouts of terror about financial crises—are all too often the result of poor or nonexistent planning, however. They shouldn't happen, and they don't have to.

The financial ups and downs of most Americans' lives are highly predictable, and in most cases, the causes of fiscal calamity aren't hard to discern. With some degree of understanding about what the future holds, both in kind (college educations, down payments on houses, and retirement) and in amount (total cost and necessary savings today), the ordinary American family and individual can face the future with confidence. With some understanding of the nature of these crossroads and how they can be anticipated, life will hold fewer terrors and far more peace of mind—at least in the financial area of the brain.

2

For most of us, life presents a series of financial issues for which we can prepare. But most of the time, the plans we make for these predictable crises are comparatively crude. We put more thought into what we'll do for our summer vacation or what car we'll buy (and use better planning tools in the process) than, say, what we'll live on after we retire. This is a serious mistake.

Many Americans still try to set something aside for a rainy day, although few of us have an accurate idea of just when that time will come, or how much rain will fall. Yet there's a wealth of data compiled over decades telling precisely what most families and individuals can expect in the way of stormy weather, and what they'll need in terms of umbrellas.

For example, most folks know that if their children want to go to college, it will be expensive and that some provision should be made in terms of saving or borrowing. But almost no one has a clear idea of just how much an education will cost at different kinds of institutions at various times in the future, despite a mountain of data on that subject for the past, present, and future. Few individuals have any idea what amount of money, put away at what rate of interest, will be necessary to pay all the expenses of attending "State" or Stanford. Despite the raft of material on this subject, the people who need the information and the information itself hardly ever meet.

Most couples starting wedded life know that raising children isn't free, but they have only a vague idea as to how much the bassinet and Pampers will set them back or, as time passes, how much car and life insurance and private school will be. They remain unaware of the actual cost of raising a child, despite the government computers filled with data on the subject, taking into account variations in economic circumstances, family size, and regions of the nation.

Most people anticipate that they'd like to retire someday. They know that it will take a certain sum of money to afford a vacation home and a membership to a country club, and they also suspect that it's foolish to count on very much from Social Security. Unfortunately, they don't have a precise idea of what their later years will cost or how much they need to put aside.

Your authors have written a book on precisely this subject: *Yes, You Can Still Retire Comfortably!* But how does saving for retirement interact with all the other events for which we have to plan throughout our lives? How does it fit into the bigger picture?

Ideally, we'd match up our projected earnings and spending over a lifetime to avoid as much money worry as possible and maximize our financial security. The American salaried worker has an opportunity to improve his or her life dramatically by making use of what economic scientists have found out about lifetime earnings and expenditures. The problem up until now has been that this information hasn't been adequately publicized and synthesized. While recent decades have seen a successful effort to explain up-to-the-minute medical research in laymen's terms, no similar effort has been made with journalism in economics. Statistics on carbohydrates and saturated fat are printed right on the packages, yet the average person is hard-pressed to find vital economic and financial statistics compiled in a comprehensive guide for the public.

If the American family or individual can take the scientific data that has been accumulated on how to maintain economic health—

3

much of the data admittedly stashed away in boring research journals—they can make just as good a use of that data as they've done with health research, in learning how to eat properly or exercise regularly.

The basic principles are quite simple and straightforward. To match up your lifetime earnings with your lifetime expenditures is no different from reconciling your income with your spending on a monthly basis—except that here we simply take a much longer view. Instead of trying to align 30 days of outgo on rent, meals, gasoline, babysitting, cosmetics, clothing, and shoes with one month's paycheck, we're doing something far more ambitious, but no less possible: matching up a lifetime's probable spending on housing, college educations, automobiles, and retirement with a lifetime's earnings from labor, investments, and interest income.

To do so, we need a road map of what the usual expenditures are for middle-class Americans and a guide for what the years may bring in the way of income. We also need to make basic projections on our investments. While it seems impossible, that's only the case for short-term investors. For those around for the long term, the probable rate of return is so sufficiently reliable that it has very tentatively been promoted to the status of a constant, called "Siegel's constant," after Professor Jeremy Siegel, author of *Stocks for the Long Run*. We know the likely after-inflation rates of return from long-term investing in cash, bonds, real estate, and stocks.

Another key to getting a financial life is something that makes a great many people queasy: borrowing. This is an essential tool for economic wellness in this world, no different from using a credit card. Borrowing isn't the path to perdition, nor is it a way to lose your reputation and your worldly goods in an orgy of uncontrollable indebtedness. Properly used, it can be indispensable for making your life work properly in the financial sphere.

The four parts of getting your financial life's crises ironed out are no more than having a general idea of:

1. How much predictable events will cost

2. How much you're likely to earn at different stages of your life

3. How much money to save and when

4. Some grasp of when and how much to borrow

Even more briefly, let's say that this book will try to tell you how much things will cost and how you might arrange to pay for them. Our purpose is to ensure that you have as few nasty surprises, jagged bouts of money anxiety, and days of miserable scrimping as humanly possible.

How We're Going to Help You Out

In the 1950s, economists created something called the "life cycle" model of financial planning. The effort was pioneered by Franco Modigliani, who won a Nobel Prize (in part) for his work developing the theory. Here's the CliffsNotes version:

As a living and breathing human being, you have a constant need for consumption throughout your entire life: food, shelter, clothing, and so on. This remains true whether you're 2 years old or 22 or 92.

5

Your ability to earn money to pay for all the things that you consume, however, isn't constant. Americans today aren't sent off to work in the mines and mills as small children—in fact, laws wisely prevent this. Most old people today don't work, either. They don't currently labor to create the stream of wealth that pays for the various resources they consume. Rather, their income is supplemented from their earlier savings, as well as from social-transfer programs arranged by the government.

Viewed from a lifetime perspective, most people find their income starting low, with part-time jobs during their school years, and then ballooning rapidly after they leave the classroom with full-time employment, then moving into middle age, when income tends to flatten out. Then, for most people, earned income tends to decline, steeply or gradually, as they begin the process of retirement.

In sum, it looks something like the highly simplified Figure 1.1.

Figure 1.1: Income and Consumption Over the Life Cycle

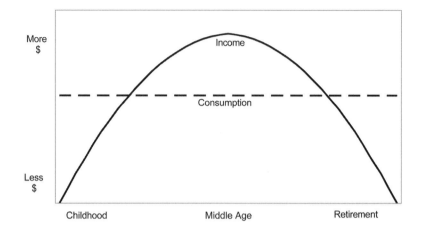

We borrow and save to keep the dotted line of consumption relatively level throughout our lifetime, in spite of the fact that our earned income (the solid, curving line) fluctuates. During childhood, when our consumption vastly exceeds our income, we take from our parents. During middle age, we try to live below our means and save some of the surplus (the area under the curve above but above the dotted line) to help fund our retirement. This is also aided by government transfers such as Medicare and Social Security.

There are two big conclusions to be drawn from this illustration. First, people want to have as *high* a line of consumption as possible. Given a choice between traveling through life in economy or first class, most people choose the latter. No Nobel Prize will be forthcoming for this observation (but we're open to it).

Second, people generally prefer to have as *smooth* a line of consumption as possible—preferably one that's sloping upward. If you've ever been fired and wondered where your next mortgage payment would come from, you'll have a keen appreciation of this fact. There's nothing quite like a sudden, precipitous drop in income to send ice water down your spine.

Less obvious is the fact that sudden jumps in income can also be disorienting. This was the whole premise of the old television program *The Millionaire,* where every week John Beresford Tipton would give away a check for a million dollars to some unsuspecting person, often with the result that the new millionaire's life would self-destruct. The stories of lottery winners are often cautionary tales in this regard as well.

Here's a basic thought: If someone gives you a million dollars today, you shouldn't spend it all tomorrow. The smart move would be to use it to raise your standard of living for the rest of your life. If you understand this, then you already grasp the basics of life cycle financial planning.

This question is a bit less basic: What if a rich aunt died and left $10 million for you in a passbook savings account that, for some technical reason, you couldn't touch for ten years. Let's further suppose you are currently 20 years old and earn $20,000 a year.

Does it really make sense to live like a comparative pauper for a whole decade—possibly some of the finest years of your life—and then become Joe Millionaire once you hit 30 and get your hands on the money? Not from the life cycle financial planning point of view. What would make more sense would be to figure out how much this windfall might be worth when considered as an annual lifetime income supplement, and then raise your present standard of living (even by borrowing against it) to give you consistently as high a lifestyle as you can afford, taking the big picture into account.

Now let's push this example one step further and get to the heart of this tome: Imagine that you could take all the big variables in your life—your career promotions, life insurance, children's education, retirement, and so on—and feed them into a computer. The calculations would also take into account the rates of return on your savings and investments, and at the same time run everything through the U.S. tax code. It could then generate a magic number that tells you exactly how much you should spend every year. This would be the highest number possible, considering all of the various financial contingencies. It would be a *sustainable* standard of living—that is, you'd be living in the real world, not being needlessly ascetic or heading down a road that leads off a cliff.

This computer exists, and we used it in writing this book. It's actually a software program called ESPlanner that can run on a home PC. It represents a ten-year labor of love on the part of two distinguished economists: Professor Laurence Kotlikoff of Boston University and Jagadeesh Gokhale of the Cato Institute. You can buy a copy for yourself for about $150, if you want to go into more detail than we provide here. You'll find a link to it (and any other Websites that we reference along the way) from your authors' own Website: **www.stein-demuth.com**.

ESPlanner allows you to enter all the particulars of your life situation and then makes its calculations to the nearest dollar. Given the inherent imprecision of some of the factors that plug into these calculations, our goal is far more modest. We want to give you answers that are generally right. When it comes to financial planning, there's a truism: It's far more important to be generally right than precisely wrong. Most people, unfortunately, haven't even gotten to a point where they're in either situation; rather, they're completely in the dark. They just try to pay the bills month to month and cross their fingers for the rest. After you read this book, you won't need to knock on wood. You'll know where you stand; you'll have a financial life.

Through life cycle financial planning, you can put bumpers and shock absorbers on your finances and smooth out your consumption at as high a level as possible. Most other approaches prescribe a fixed rate of saving and then let your consumption (that is, your lifestyle) swing wildly up and down in order to maintain the steady savings. This is the tail wagging the dog.

Life cycle planning starts by keeping your consumption as constant and high as possible, and then varies your recommended savings to achieve a level field on which to live and play. This makes more sense.

In making lifelong projections, one of the issues you'll face is that you can't know how much you're able to spend until you know what your taxes are going to be . . . but you won't be able to figure out your taxes until you determine how much you're going to be saving or spending in each given year. Try calculating this on your own and you'll chew your pencil to a nub. But ESPlanner handles this with aplomb.

Here's an example that gives you only one idea of its prestidigitation:

> . . . the program's federal income tax calculator decides if the household should itemize deductions, whether it is eligible for the earned-income and child-tax credits, and the extent to which its Social Security benefits are subject to taxation. It also includes the Alternative Minimum Tax. And it takes into account the most recent changes in federal and state income tax provisions. The state income tax calculator incorporates the progressive rate structure, deductions, and exemptions in each state's income tax law. (ESPlanner Tutorial, p. 4)

In other words, there's a lot to this.

◆

You may find the whole idea of taking charge of your financial life frightening. After all, money can be a terrifying subject. When you confront an issue that's this basic to your life, instead of running away from it, you'll find that, paradoxically, it sets you free.

People often flee from taking responsibility for their financial lives because it's such a big subject. But after a point, they're afraid simply *because* they're running. This book will help you stop, turn around, and confront head-on the financial challenges that face you. Not the imaginary fears of your worst nightmares, but the real issues before you.

When you do so, you'll gain courage that will sustain you in many areas of your life. You'll be facing these financial hurdles eventually, one way or another, and sooner is better. You'll find it easier by far to have a plan such as we lay out in this book than to be sitting scared in the dark.

Before we launch into the particulars, a few words are in order for young people about some crucial things they can do to raise the income that they'll earn in their lifetimes. This is the subject of Chapter 2.

◤◥◤

MAXIMIZE YOUR LIFETIME WEALTH

H orrible though it is to contemplate, the decisions we make as teenagers can have the single biggest impact on our lifetime wealth. While our culture worships young people, and TV shows and movies routinely show them as being smarter, hipper, and, above all, wiser than the doltish adults around them, it's nevertheless the case that teens are capable of making notoriously bad decisions—some with long-lasting implications.

The corollary of this is that many of the things our grandparents told us, which we flippantly ignored at the time, actually prove to be extremely shrewd advice. The trick to being a successful teenager is to try to get as many of these big things right as we can, along with whatever mistakes we (unavoidably) will make along the way.

Be of Good Character

One very important thing that you can do to influence your lifetime wealth is to be a person of good character. By this we mean someone who's honest, trustworthy, reliable, and hardworking.

Being truthful is the key to winning the confidence of others. In fact, we'd go so far as to say that in our experience, the more successful people are, the more forthcoming they usually are about owning up to their shortcomings. They're willing to admit their mistakes, even when the truth is painful. Dishonest folks usually have something to hide (often from themselves). Their underhandedness catches up with them, and they're soon marginalized and don't get to play at the tables where the successful people are.

Work involves trust. If you aren't a person who can be trusted even when there's $100 sitting in the petty-cash box, there's no one in the office, you could really use some extra money to impress your date this weekend, and your chances of being caught are nil, the bitter truth is that you'll be one of life's losers. We don't pretend to understand how it works, but people who break the rules always seem to end up in dead-end jobs, and eventually with *no* job.

The same is true for people who are unreliable. If you don't show up when you say you're going to, you have little value to an employer. If your word doesn't mean anything, then neither, likely, will you. You may have many abilities that have value in the marketplace—you may even have the skill to carry a football ten yards without being tackled. But unless you show up for practice regularly and work extremely hard, it won't make a difference. You'll just be hanging out on the street corner watching life pass by . . . and no one will hand you the football.

Of course, there are some people who have a lot of money in spite of their bad, even criminal behavior, but these are exceptions. Trying to be like one of them is a strategy with almost no chance of success.

Go to College, Get Some Knowledge

The next thing you need is a college education. The further you go with your education, the better it will be for you later on—even if, in the short run, it seems like the kids who dropped out of high school to work in the hair salon or body shop have more spending money on weekends. Figure 2.1, containing 2003 data courtesy of the Federal Reserve Bank of Dallas, eloquently tells the tale:

Figure 2.1: Lifetime Earnings by Educational Attainment

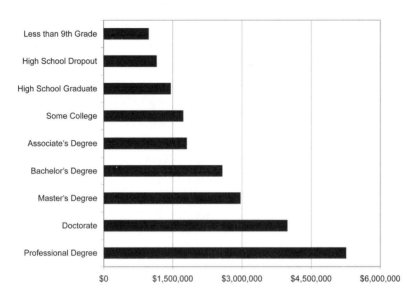

Get the picture? A person with a professional degree has more than five times the lifetime earnings of someone who never went to high school. So what if the average student leaves college with $19,000 worth of debt and the average graduate student leaves grad school with $31,000 in educational loans hanging over his or her head? From the point of view of lifetime financial planning, this is the best money he or she will ever spend.

Employers will want you more if you have valuable, specialized skills—that is, those that will help them solve a problem. The harder these skills are to acquire and the more important they are to your potential employer's cash flow, the better off you'll be. If someone can sum up everything there is to know about a job in 15 minutes, it probably won't be a very high-paying position. For this reason, courses that have difficult-to-acquire content, such as those that require mathematics and the sciences, are likely to lead to a better outcome for you. Of course, these are the classes that young people try to avoid, because they are harder than, say, courses in anthropology or sociology. But it's precisely because they're more difficult that the students who master these subjects usually have brighter career prospects later on.

Any college graduate, however, has demonstrated that he or she is capable of showing up, sitting still, and following directions, as well as having some ability to talk, write, and analyze. These skills will qualify you for a meaningful place in the workforce.

Beyond this, according to Joseph Epstein's book *Snobbery,* there are approximately 20 colleges that, if you can gain access to their ivied halls, may stand to give you some special (if indeterminate) advantage in life. These are:

Amherst	Dartmouth	Univ. of Michigan	Univ. of Virginia
Brown	Duke	Northwestern	Wellesley
Berkeley	Georgetown	Princeton	Wesleyan
Univ. of Chicago	Harvard	Smith	Williams
Columbia	Johns Hopkins	Stanford	Yale

The superiority of these schools, at least at the undergraduate level, doesn't seem to issue from the education they provide, but rather from the competitive entrance ordeal and the resulting high IQ of the student body. Nevertheless, if you're fortunate enough to attend one of these schools, one of the most important books you'll open there will be your Rolodex. The friendships that you make will stand to be of service to you for your entire life. Naturally, there are no guarantees. We know plenty of people who went to these schools who have made next to nothing of the opportunity.

We might as well say it now: Connections in life are essential. Almost everything good that comes your way will happen as the result of some personal association. While doors may open for you because you fill out an application and mail in a résumé, more often than not it will be because you happen to know somebody who knows somebody who happens to be the key person. Of course, once you have the opportunity, then it's up to you to deliver. But connections are the equivalent of somebody handing you the football. Without them, you might as well be on the bench.

14

Appearance Counts

You know how we're constantly being admonished not to judge by appearances? The reason for this is simple: Everyone judges by appearances. No one can see into your soul. If we had to judge every person according to his or her unique merits and demerits, we'd never get past square one. So people go by what they see, and usually do so within a matter of milliseconds. In our experience, we find that appearances are mainly, if not infallibly, correct (but for an important exception involving young women with big breasts and young men with BMWs, see pages 30–31).

Now that you know that people will judge you by how you look, you can convert this information into ammunition. You can arm yourself to gain a competitive advantage over those poor slobs who haven't figured this out.

Neatness counts, and so does being appropriately dressed. Unless you're applying for a job playing rhythm guitar with the Rolling Stones, having tattoos and body piercings is unlikely to be an asset in most employment situations.

15

Has anyone outside of the bedroom ever commented on your cologne or perfume? If so, it means that you're wearing way too much and should throw the bottle away immediately, even if you paid $10 for it.

Social psychologists have established that good-looking people have a tremendous advantage over those who are unattractive. You may not look like Hugh Grant or Salma Hayek, but anything reasonable you can do to avoid looking like Jabba the Hutt will help.

All this means that you should strive to make a good first impression. Once you've done so, it's very inconvenient for someone to change his mind later. If you get an A on your first English paper, the professor will assume that you're smart and you're very likely to get all A's thereafter, because it saves him the trouble of actually having to read your papers. What's more, you'll soon get the reputation for being an A student in general, and it will be very difficult for anyone in the humanities to give you a lesser grade.

Microsoft

Whether you're a high-school dropout or a multi-degreed professional, you must become computer literate. By computer, we mean PC, not Mac, and more briefly still, we mean Microsoft. Today's young people should learn their way around Windows and know how to use MS Word, Excel, PowerPoint, and Internet Explorer.

A high-school dropout of our acquaintance happened to take a course to become a Microsoft-certified technician. This is the very Platonic form of acquiring specialized, valuable skills. He now earns a six-figure salary running a corporate IT department.

While we're on the subject of software, it will be extremely helpful if you get in the habit of entering your financial transactions into either Intuit's Quicken or Microsoft's Money. These two programs seem to go neck and neck in terms of superiority, with each new version slightly eclipsing its rival's previous effort. Using either one will put you light-years ahead of the person who has neither. It takes a little more time to get set up and to do the data entry each month (although increasingly this is a matter of downloading account information from the Internet), but it more than pays you back in terms of the peace of mind that comes from standing atop your financial pyramid rather than being crushed beneath it. The extra time you invest will be repaid instantly on April 15th, when you gather your previous year's tax information with the click of a button and export it into a tax preparation program, instead of spending days looking for lost checks and missing statements.

Graduate School

Grad students are forever complaining about their lot in life and the professors who don't appreciate their genius. It's true that graduate students are typically expected to do two weeks' worth of work every semester, unlike undergraduates, who usually can get by with one week's work or less. If you do go to grad school, in spite of all your complaining at the time, someday you'll look back on your stint and realize that it was very heaven (to borrow from Wordsworth, whom we read in high school).

Once you finish your studies, you'll probably have gigantic college debts to pay. Be sure to consolidate them all into one low, fixed-rate loan. Stretch them out from here to eternity. The subsidies in effect here will assure that this will be some of the cheapest money you ever borrow.

Job One

A few pointers about your first grown-up gig. To get the job, use your family connections for everything they're worth. While it's less threatening to mail in a résumé to a post-office box, a personal contact will get you in the door. Résumés are used to screen people out, not in, so make sure yours doesn't offer any reason for a person not to interview you. Misspellings and grammatical mistakes are extremely common and instant disqualifiers. They get passed around the office for laughs.

If you show up dressed appropriately, look the interviewer in the eye, and shake his or her hand firmly, you will place yourself in the top 10 percent of applicants. It goes without saying (but we'll say it anyway) that you don't use profanity in your job interview, and while, like, it might be all about how, like, totally awesome it would be to, you know, get the job, dude, avoid using slang as well. Profanity and slang immediately lower your IQ in the eyes of others.

At the job interview—and from this point forward and forevermore—there's one thing to keep in mind: It's not about you; it's entirely about them. It's about what you can do for the company. This means that you should be as knowledgeable as possible about what it does.

Do your homework—annual reports and Google come to mind. Learn as much as you can about the person who will be interviewing you. If you can discover that he happens to be a tiddlywinks champion, you have a factoid to exploit in your conversation, giving you an instant edge over those applicants who didn't go to

17

this trouble. There's no law against calling people in the company whom you might be working with and asking them about the issues they're facing. That way, in the interview, you can sound like you're ready to hit the ground running, instead of being the clueless new guy they'll have to wise up.

Above all, you should be the kind of person whom anyone would want to work with. Bright, smiling, enthusiastic, eager to get started, and willing to work hard to do a great job. A person who unquestionably will represent the company well, and who will add value to the whole enterprise.

Don't even think of letting a day go by after your initial meeting without sending the interviewer a personalized, legible, handwritten (but brief) thank-you note on nice stationery. A plain note card from Crane will do nicely. Thank the interviewer for his or her time and consideration. Say that you're excited about the prospect of working for Acme, how it feels like a great fit for you, and how much you look forward to making a contribution.

Did you perhaps talk to more than one person during your visit? Send each of them an individualized card. No one else will bother, so you'll be the one they talk about among themselves. To do this, you should try to note something personal about each interviewer, and get their business cards. A pleasant appearance, an enthusiastic disposition, and a thank-you note follow-up are extremely potent job-getting tools.

Once you land the job, you'll probably feel like an impostor for the first week. Everyone else will be walking around, apparently knowing what's going on, and you'll have no idea what you're doing there. This is the universal experience, and the solution is to fake it till you make it.

In fact, the basic answer to all job-related questions is this: You've been hired to make your boss look good. This is the way of the world. There's no Supreme Court that metes out fairness; there's only your arbitrary and capricious boss. If you make your boss look good (yes, this means giving him or her all the credit for your hard work), guess who benefits? You do.

The final point is to make yourself indispensable. Be the first to arrive and the last to leave, especially at the beginning, when you're making the only first impression that you will get to make. Understand how what you do relates to the organization's ability to make money. If you work for a profitable company and you add value for your employer in excess of the expense of your salary and benefits, you'll never have to worry about losing your job. On the other hand, if you don't add more than you cost, there will be no such thing as job security.

Play Well with Others

The final job skill is to get along with others. People who don't fit in get moved to the sidelines as the great caravan of economic progress moves forward.

Screenwriter John Hill tells of the disappointment he faced when he graduated from college and started working at an advertising agency. In college, every semester brought a new shuffling of classes and coeds, an exciting mix of new people to meet and date. But after graduation, at the ad agency, something unexpected happened. The seasons changed, but the people stayed the same. Month after month, year after year, he saw the same faces all the time, every day.

There's an important lesson here: Don't date someone in your office. If you do, every intimate detail of your romantic life will become known to everyone at work. There will be no secrets. When it blows up, the whole affair will prove to be a humiliating disaster. In fact, no matter where you meet them, treat your dating partners with respect, before, during, and after. Strive to minimize collateral damage and casualties from friendly fire. Be gracious in victory and defeat.

(Perhaps marital advice is out of place in a book about personal finance, so forgive us if we overstep. But a quick word to the wise: If someone is high maintenance, either emotionally or financially—and they often go together—you have to ask whether you can afford to have this person in your life in the long run. Don't marry someone who expects you to spend a lot of money on him or her just because he or she showed up. Let someone else have the opportunity.)

A final point of professionalism: Use your work e-mail address for work-related correspondence only, and keep your hard drive clean. Don't ever write anything in an e-mail that you wouldn't want published in *The New York Times*.

Now that your career is launched, let's consider what lies ahead for your 20s. . . .

◤◥◤

CHAPTER 3

IN YOUR 20S

Productivity and You

Let us pause briefly to meditate on Figure 3.1, a chart of great beauty, marvelous to behold. It shows what happens to the income of men and women during the decade of their 20s. This is the latest data from the U.S. Census Bureau, from 2001.

Figure 3.1: Inflation-Adjusted Income in Your 20s

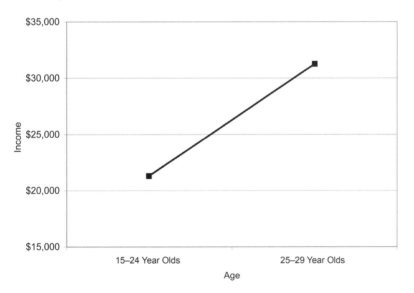

The trend line is unambiguous: Income rises dramatically during the first years of a career. This is why it's important to seize upon that blessed time as the launchpad for a financially secure tomorrow. True, getting your act together in the first decade of work isn't indispensable, just as being born as a Rockefeller is not absolutely necessary. But in both cases, the money will come in handy. If you correctly manage the opportunities that this rising income stream presents, you'll find that, in effect, you've given yourself a trust fund to draw upon for the rest of your life.

Your income doesn't rise in your 20s just because you're young. In fact, your increasing salary is the result of market forces that have nothing to do with you, per se.

To understand why, think of yourself as an employer. You own the Pygmy Athletic Shoe Company, and you have an office where you handle the incoming orders for athletic shoes before sending them to the factory. Along comes Jane Q. Colgrad, a recent graduate of the local junior college. Jane is a personable, intelligent woman of 21. She seems peppy and willing to work.

Unfortunately, she knows zero about the athletic-shoe business. She was clever enough to wear Pygmies to her job interview and rave about how great they are, which, to be honest, is why you hired her. But she knows nothing about your company in particular. She doesn't understand how to use your computer system beyond playing solitaire, nor does she know the names and idiosyncrasies of your salespeople and their customers, your accounting system, your database, or really anything that would be immediately useful to you. However, she's eager and willing to learn, and you need somebody.

In her first year at the office, Jane makes a great many mistakes. She accidentally erases a crucial computer file, and you learn that your backup system isn't as good as it was supposed to be, so work grinds to a halt for a week while you tediously re-create the file by manually reentering and checking all the data. She neglects to send checks to the bank the very minute they come in, thereby losing interest. She forgets that a certain salesman wants to have a specific kind of rental car when he travels the territory around Palm Springs. She puts your biggest account on hold for ten minutes because she doesn't want to interrupt you while you're talking to the copier repairman. In your darker moments, you fear that you made a mistake in hiring her.

But then, little by little, she learns. The athletic-shoe business isn't really that complicated when you get down to it, and a smart gal like Jane Q. Colgrad can pick it up at a basic level within a couple of years. By the end of the first year, she's had an intense course in the athletic-shoe business. In particular, she's had a crash course in *your* specific business, which now makes her worth quite a lot. Whatever you started paying her at the beginning is nowhere near enough any longer, so you give her a good raise. Then, after the second year, she knows the business better than all but a few Pygmy veterans. You begin to get scared that Jane Q. Colgrad could leave and take her skills with her to the Maori Athletic Shoe Company across town. You give her a really excellent pay increase after that, just to keep her heart in the right place.

By her third year, she remembers the name of every salesperson's spouse. She knows her way around the latest version of the software far better than you do. She's taken your banking completely paperless, which made you nervous at first, but she seems to manage effortlessly with just a few clicks. In fact, Jane has become a key part of the whole enterprise. You, her employer, realize that she's vital to the successful running of the office. At this point, Pygmy would be in deep trouble if she weren't there.

23

At the end of that third year, Florence, the office manager who's been with you since you started Pygmy, retires, and Jane takes her place. If she left now and you had to train someone else, the sales office would be in chaos for a year. You give her another raise in pay.

After the fourth year, she meets the founder of the Maori athletic-shoe company. When he talks to Jane Q. Colgrad, he realizes that she knows the business the way a dog knows sleeping. He offers her a management-level position at Maori. Jane Q. Colgrad comes to you and says that she's sorry, because she really loves the Pygmy people, but she wouldn't be fair to herself if she didn't take the big step up at Maori.

Your heart sinks. You tell her that the competitor's products are a passing fad. She might be making the mistake of her life if she leaves Pygmy. Besides, how much is Maori going to give her? Pygmy has had a good year and might just be able to meet the offer. Jane Q. Colgrad walks out of the office with a management-level position at Pygmy and a fat pay increase.

This is an idealized schematic of how life works. To be sure, there are bosses who will tell you to get lost if you say that you're going to a rival. There are also managers who are so ignorant of the workings of business that they won't pay anything extra for your fine work and your new skills and knowledge. And there are companies that are suffering so badly from recessions, foreign competition, or inept management that they simply can't afford to pay a sizable wage increase.

But by and large, as the young worker starts at a position, figures out how the business works, and makes him- or herself invaluable to employers, the pay rises dramatically. Since most businesses aren't terribly complicated, most of what needs to be learned can be mastered fairly quickly. The employee's increase in skill and knowledge is quickly translated into productivity increases. As this happens, employers will pay more—not out of any inherent generosity or kindness of heart, but strictly because the employee is worth more in the marketplace.

24

The curve of increased learning and skill tilts very sharply upward in the first years of work because your productivity increases aggressively as well. Your pay rises rapidly as you learn the ropes and become worth far more to your employer.

Happy Days

Now for the expenditure side. Of course, spending can and will vary wildly from person to person. Some people will live at home with Mom and Dad for several years after they begin their first post-school job. They may take the bus to work, brown-bag it for lunch, and go on vacation with their parents at the old cabin in the mountains or just not go at all. For those individuals, expenditures will rise only slowly above what they were back in the day when the worker was in school.

There will be other folks who will take their first paycheck and get an apartment in a gentrified neighborhood. With the second paycheck, they'll make the down payment on a complete set of furniture. With the third, they'll lease a 3-series BMW. For these people, expenditures will shoot up hopelessly.

But the ordinary twentysomething entering the job market will take a middle course. There will be expenditures for the young person's own or shared dwelling, usually for a (used) car, and for a very substantial increase in the amount and quality of clothing. There will be a large jump in the cost of "food eaten away from home," as statisticians call meals at restaurants. There will also be noticeable growth in the cost of vacations.

Unfortunately, the rising income at work leads to a sense of psychological inflation, the idea that there will always be enough money tomorrow to cover one's consumption today. We see this kind of narcissism all over Hollywood: Who cares about how much I run up in the way of Visa bills? Pretty soon I'll land that part (or sell that script or direct that feature), and I'll be the next Keanu Reeves, and it will be a trivial matter to pay it off.

The problem is that for every Keanu Reeves, there are 50,000 actors who don't become Keanu Reeves, but whose bills come due just the same. Psychologically, if you're inclined to say "I'll pay for it tomorrow" when you're in your 20s, you're predisposed to say the same thing in your 30s, 40s, and 50s. And eventually you're staring at an old age of poverty and despair because you have no savings.

The young man thinks that old age is something that happens to other people, but that *he* will live fast, die young, and leave a beautiful corpse (buried with a Fender Stratocaster by his side). The last thing he wants to hear is that one day he'll be like his parents or his grandparents.

The make-a-dollar, spend-a-dollar mentality is reinforced by the idea that you're finally free from all parental control and can now do whatever you want. If you live in an anonymous city instead of a small town, no one will know or care what you're up to. Young people are constantly exposed to advertisements, TV shows, and movies that show 20-year-olds wearing Prada, driving Porsches, and living like pashas. If they are, why not you—aren't you equally deserving?

Add credit cards to this combustible mixture, and it gets scary. Given the psychological factors at work, it isn't surprising to learn that people who use home-equity lines to pay off their credit cards—a seemingly smart move—end up with credit-card bills just as high a year later.

If you do dig yourself into a black hole of debt, be aware that most of the places you go to help yourself get out are themselves running some kind of scam to prey upon the desperate and helpless. Debtors Anonymous (**www.debtorsanonymous.org**) is the major exception. There's also legitimate debt counseling to be had at the National Foundation for Credit Counseling (**www.nfcc.org**).

How Not to Borrow Trouble

In general, it doesn't make sense to borrow money to purchase depreciating assets. It does make sense to borrow to increase your human capital, such as acquiring specialized skills that have value in the marketplace. A college diploma or a professional degree leap instantly to mind here. It's also wise to borrow money to buy a home if the house otherwise fits within your budget (lots more on this later).

Borrowing money from Infiniti to buy a G35 or from Visa to buy an Ermenegildo Zegna suit (unless you religiously pay off your balance in full every month) makes less sense. These items will plummet in value the minute you take them out of the showroom.

If you ignore our warnings and decide to borrow anyway, any short-term loans should be used for something necessary, and arranged in such a way that the repayment can be accomplished quickly. For example, a young man or woman in his or her first apartment shouldn't be expected to crawl into a sleeping bag each night or to entertain guests on orange crates. In a society like the United States, under ordinary circumstances, a young member of the labor force can buy furniture. This person will also need a sensible wardrobe to get to work in a presentable fashion.

If you must borrow to get these items, then so be it. Just make repaying your credit-card debt a high priority thereafter. It's impossible to have a financial life that makes sense while you're throwing 21 percent interest to the hounds of the credit industry month after month.

At the Bank

It may be that you'll need to go into a bank in order to borrow at some point in your young life, and there are a few simple principles that should govern your conduct in asking for a loan. Remember that most bank lending officers are just people like you. They want very much to get through the day without any unnecessary aggravation. If their job is to make loans, they want to follow the bank guidelines and not get themselves in trouble. They have no feelings about you personally, so don't confuse them with your uncle or your best friend. They absolutely won't lend to you because they like your face or your smile, but they will do so if you meet their criteria. It's that simple.

Put yourself in the loan officer's place. Would you grant someone funds if you might lose your job should the deal go sour? Try to find out what the institution's specifications are for getting the loan in question, and then try to meet those specs. Remember, banks live and die by making loans, so they don't want to turn down an application. The general idea is to work with them in a joint venture to get the loan. The process shouldn't be a confrontation or an opportunity for you to ventilate your grievances against the exploitative capitalist system and its lackey bankers.

Lenders generally base their decision about you and your loan on what's still called the three C's: *collateral, creditworthiness, and character.* It's sad to say, but in this mass society, your character is usually unknown to your banker, and it isn't considered. Gone are the days shown in *It's a Wonderful Life* and *The Best Years of Our Lives* when the banker would size you up and give you a loan based on whether he liked the cut of your jib. What's more, when you're starting out in adult life, your collateral is likely to be nil. But you still can show creditworthiness—the ability to repay the loan.

As a general rule, the bank wants to see that if you lump all of your installment debt together, it won't exceed 25 percent of your pretax income. (This doesn't include mortgage debt.) If you aren't going to be able to show that, you should have a good explanation. When you fill out the forms, you should try to arrange the data so that you're able to meet that 25 percent rule. This doesn't mean fudging the papers. It does mean that you should be alert to what's considered the margin of safety for repaying loans—for your sake and the bank's.

What's Your Number?

You can spare yourself a lot of potential embarrassment by knowing your FICO score before you go loan shopping. You can find it out at **www.myfico.com** or for free at **www.annualcredit report.com**. Check your report carefully for any errors that may have crept in, and realize that it may take some time and patience— and plenty of correspondence—to correct them.

Where does your FICO score come from? It's a formula creditors have developed for predicting their likelihood of being repaid if they lend you money. The factors that go into measuring your creditworthiness are pretty obvious: They want to see that you have a history of repaying your bills in full and on time, you have a stable job and living situation, your credit cards aren't all maxed out, you haven't declared bankruptcy, and so on. If your credit cards are at even 50 percent of their limits, that counts against you, as does opening a bunch of new credit cards.

If you have no credit history or only a short one, that's also a negative. These agencies want to see that you can successfully handle what's been given to you over time, and preferably several different types: a credit card, car loan, mortgage, home-equity loans, and so on. But the basics are not maxing out your cards and paying your bills in full and on time.

FICO scores range from 300 to 850, with higher being better. The median (50th percentile) score is 600, and if you can boost your number to 720, then you'll usually qualify for loans on the most favorable terms, because you'll have proven yourself to be a good risk. If your credit score is below 720, you'll have to pay lenders a higher rate of interest to compensate them for what they believe will be the greater risk associated with lending you money. The difference between having a high score or a low one can cost you thousands of dollars a year in mortgage-interest payments alone.

What's more, credit scores are increasingly being used as a quick and dirty check on you for a variety of purposes for which they were never intended. Will you make a good, reliable employee? Are you a sound risk to insure? Because it's such an easy way for others to get a quick snapshot of how "risky" you are, it pays to make sure that your numbers are as high as possible.

Shopping Around

If you're in the market for a loan, don't make the mistake of thinking that all of them are equal. They can cost wildly different amounts of interest and origination fees. The difference over a four-year loan for a new car can be many thousands of dollars. Momma told you to shop around, and it was good advice, since banks can and do compete on rates. It's often the best-paid hour of your life to surf the Web to find where you can get the best deal. A good place to start is **www.bankrate.com**.

Banks should always be the first place to look for a loan (after calling Mom and Dad). Their rates are almost always lower than those at finance companies, less than what you'll pay the furniture store or the appliance center, and unbelievably cheaper than the interest you'll pay on credit-card debt.

In your 20s, you're in a period of high income growth, but you're starting from a low base. If you only burden yourself with the smallest possible interest payments, you'll have the widest possible gap between what you earn and what you spend. This will give you the maximum savings with which to meet the easily foreseen financial pitfalls that are coming down the pike of life.

Keeping the Lid On

If we take a dim view of borrowing without collateral, we take an even dimmer view of overspending. *Don't I have a right to enjoy the same things that others seem to have?* you may wonder. The bitter truth is that you're only entitled to have what an honest accounting says you can afford. The key difference between people who are able to save and those who aren't is that the former are able to do without vanity and status items.

Cars, furniture, vacations, and recreation expenses—the items that allow young people to display their wealth and their prestige—are also the things that can wreck the possibility of saving. Many people consider extravagance a sin, but morality has little to do with the laws of economics. If you can save while driving a Bentley Continental, more power to you.

We once knew a woman who went to a "personal-growth" workshop. There, she learned that rich people carry ostrich-skin designer wallets that cost $600. Although she was broke, she put a $600 wallet on her credit card to channel rich people's energy *(prana)* her way. To become wealthy, she thought that she had only to act like a rich person, and the money would flow to her by cosmic law. She did; it didn't.

One of the reasons why young adults spend so much on restaurants, alcohol, clothing, and cars is because they're out in the dating marketplace, looking for potential long-term partners to marry or otherwise settle down with for the duration. Being the superficial creatures that human beings are, we naturally want the most high-status partners we can find: the most powerful and athletic males, the most symmetrical and harmoniously rounded females. In other words, we're looking for the best providers and potential parents.

In courtship, romantic prospects present themselves in the best possible light (notoriously, as being better than they really are) so that by the time the new partner figures out the truth, he or she is already locked into the relationship sufficiently and will overlook the newly discovered defects. This is why Ben Franklin advised people to keep their eyes wide open before marriage and half-closed afterward.

Given this big picture and the high stakes, might it be rational for a young man to lease a BMW convertible, even if he can't really afford it, in order to increase his chances of mating and marrying well, or for a young woman to spend money on breast-augmentation surgery?

Let's be frank: The young man who pulls up in a BMW is more likely to get a second look from a table of ladies than the one arriving in a beat-up Geo. And the gal with the exaggerated physique will certainly attract more stares from men. So they start out with the clear advantage that they're more likely to be noticed.

However, solving one problem can create others. If you've successfully fooled someone who wouldn't otherwise be attracted to you, you may simply have postponed the day of reckoning. When the man with the BMW can't afford to take his date to Paris for the weekend or otherwise continue to fuel a relationship with the high-octane expectations that his expensive car has engendered, he may have a lot of backpedaling to do. When the person dating the girl with the big bosoms discovers that she isn't necessarily a cornucopia of love and nurturance, or an all-bountiful sex goddess as Miss December appears to be, a sense of deflation may follow. An observer might even wonder: Was there, perhaps, some psychological deficiency that led these upwardly striving relationship seekers to pursue such expediencies in the first place?

In the long run, the guy who drives the car he can afford and the girl who lives with the breasts she already has may have an edge—the advantage of being real. They might have a harder time getting noticed, but once they've sorted each other out from the pack, they should find that the relationship is smooth sailing. Meanwhile, the guy with the BMW he can't afford will probably end up with the girl with the plastic breasts.

The temptation to overspend in your 20s is nearly overwhelming. Wise is the young adult who doesn't fall into this particular Venus flytrap. The secret is to keep your fixed expenses low (rent and car payments); not go overboard on clothing, cocktails, and dining out; remember that this goes double for vacations and furniture; and finally, handle credit cards as if they were made of kryptonite, with the power to destroy you.

Finding a roommate will cut your housing expenses considerably, while buying a reliable used car will help your transportation dollars go further. Packing your lunch and avoiding $4 coffee-flavored drinks at Starbucks will also do wonders for your budget, as will vacationing at state parks instead of on the Champs-Élysées and buying your furniture at Ikea instead of Roche-Bobois. Use a debit card instead of a credit card, even if it means passing up "free"

31

air miles. Anything you can do to clamp down on the expenditure side will pay dividends later.

The trick is to manage your affairs so that you can save during this vital decade when your income is rising so dramatically. Your 20s offer you a precious opportunity—don't blow it by pretending to the guys in the neighboring cubicles that you can afford a Range Rover. If you can avoid buying yourself into permanent indebtedness, you'll then be able to build the foundation for meeting the giant expenses that you have coming up.

Saving and Investing

The flip side of overspending and its real hidden damage is forgoing the opportunity to save. It's not the closet full of shoes that's the problem, it's the lack of an IRA. This missed opportunity, painless and invisible at the time, will nevertheless lead to huge problems later in life. Today a whole generation is entering retirement with insufficient savings. How will these people fare? No one knows. For many of them, it's not going to be pleasant.

Money saved in your 20s has a marvelous power to grow and compound over time, as the dividends, coupons, and interest are reinvested. This doesn't add up to much in the short term, but over the long term, the consequences are miraculous. And if you don't start saving now, there may not be a long term. Wait until your 40s and all you've got is a short term, and the only way to grow your savings is by Herculean self-denial.

Look at Table 3.1 to see how much we think you should save.

Table 3.1: Recommended Savings Rates as % of Current Gross Salary		
If You Have in Savings:	**You Should Save:**	
	Age 25	**Age 30**
No Retirement Savings	7%	10%
Savings = ¼ of Salary	6%	8%
Savings = ½ of Salary	4%	6%
Savings = 1 Year's Salary	1%	3%
Savings = 2 Years' Salary	0%	0%

In practice, those who haven't saved early almost never catch up. At the age of 50, a person has to save a gigantic percentage of his or her salary to have a shot at accumulating a decent nest egg by retirement. It isn't much fun, and the spouse and kids won't like it much either. But at age 25, this individual might achieve the same results by saving 7 percent of his or her current salary in a retirement account. And it gets better: When that 25-year-old turns 50, he or she still only needs to salt away 7 percent. The rest of the salary goes a long way toward buying things that grown-ups like: foreign travel, luxury automobiles, college educations for their children, and so on. Start saving when you're in your 20s and you'll be miles and smiles ahead of everyone else.

33

Naturally, Table 3.1 (and those like it in later chapters) makes a number of assumptions:

- Your portfolio will grow at a rate that's in line with historical averages for the asset classes employed.

- It's costing you about one percent annually in expenses, total (such as the expense ratios for the funds in your retirement account).

- Your career path will have your income growing in a typical fashion for someone who works full-time throughout the year.

- You'll be able to maintain your postretirement standard of living on about 84 percent of your preretirement income (as the latest studies suggest).

- Social Security will make no contribution to your income due to "means testing" once you're old and rich enough to retire.

- You don't have a pension that will be funding your retirement.

- You'll retire at age 70.

- You'll be able to draw down your nest egg at a fairly conservative rate to cover a 25-year retirement with reasonable safety.

- You follow our suggested asset allocation in your portfolio as you go along (more on this later).

34

With so many assumptions involved about an event such a long way off, there's a lot of indeterminacy in these calculations. However, you have to start somewhere, and these are as good a set of estimates as we've seen. If we come across a better one, we'll post it on our Website.

Table 3.2 tells you what a prudent young person ideally should have in the way of retirement savings (here expressed as a percentage of current salary) in order for his or her retirement account to be on track toward reaching the goal of retiring at age 70 with no Social Security, no pension, and no drop in standard of living.

Table 3.2: Are Your Retirement Savings on Track? Multiple of Current Salary You Should Have in Savings	
Age	Retirement Savings
25	0 – 0.3
30	0.3 – 0.5

In other words, a 30-year-old who earns $30,000 should ideally have somewhere between (.3 x $30,000 =) $9,000 and (.5 x $30,000 =) $15,000 invested toward the day that he or she stops working.

The amount you should have in your retirement accounts rises steeply over time, as you'll be both increasing the dollar amount you contribute (as your salary rises), as well as having compound interest work its magic on the money already saved. If your account holds less than what we specify, you should consider increasing your contributions until you catch up. Making up the difference will become harder the longer you put it off. Wait long enough, and it becomes like running through quicksand.

Simple Dreams

For the decade of your 20s, there need only be a few general guidelines:

35

- Bear in mind that the phenomenon of rapidly rising income won't continue forever.

- You'll be given every opportunity to get into serious debt with credit cards, installment plans, car leases, and the like. Screwing up here will cast a long shadow over your financial future, while a modicum of self-restraint will do wonders to provide you with a launchpad for the rest of your life.

- Now is the time to provide some foundational savings: for your retirement, emergencies, and the house and children that are likely to materialize eventually.

In other words, don't spend every cent you make when you begin work. Start a program of savings to put your financial life on rails.

◤◥◤

CHAPTER 4

SAVING AND INVESTING IN YOUR 20S

Get Rich Quick?

Into every life comes the need to try to get rich quick. A friend starts a software company. Should you put up a few thousand to get in on the deal? A pal says he's already made money on a hot new stock that he just bought. Should you buy, too? You overhear some rich guys on the golf course talking about a killing they're making in a limited partnership. Is it time to open your wallet?

The answer is simple: Never, ever speculate with money that you have some better use for, that you know you'll need. Never put funds down on anything illiquid if there's even a remote chance that you'll need to get your cash out in a hurry. For example, do not go into illiquid limited partnerships or land deals, expecting to be able to get real money out when you need it. Never, ever go into deals you don't understand. The IRS will see through them like plate glass and will make your life miserable, while the promoter will live in Rio de Janeiro on your cash.

We all want to get rich quick, but for most people, that wish only leads to sorrow. You must know that the money you put up for these schemes has only a remote likelihood of making you wealthy, but has a very real possibility of making you poor if you invest too much of it. Some people don't believe in hard work, saving, and investing, being more interested in finding the right gimmick to make them rich. We don't say that no one has ever succeeded in such endeavors; we only know that it hasn't happened to us, and we predict that it won't happen to you.

This means that you should only invest whatever you can afford to lose in speculations. For most people, given the necessity of self-funding the bulk of their retirement, that amount is easy to calculate: $0. If you think you can afford $5 a week for lottery tickets, that's like saying you can afford to throw away $1,000 every four years. Compound that amount over the next four decades and you'll see how expensive the habit can be.

The problem with uninformed speculation is that it almost always ends up having a return of minus 100 percent. You have your eye on the stratospheric prize, but you discount the astronomical risks you're taking along the way. Because both seem like big numbers, you tend to mentally equilibrate them (this is the psychological con), but they aren't equal at all. To see the difference, go to Las Vegas and look at all the beautiful casinos. They were built with the difference between what people spent at the tables and what they got back in return.

The essential paradigm shift is to move from ignorant speculating to informed investing. The sooner you can get your head wrapped around this, the wealthier you're likely to become in this life. When you invest money, you only want to take on an amount of risk that is commensurate with your expected return.

Here's one way of looking at the problem: As an investor, you're being paid to assume risk. If you keep your money in a checking account, you aren't taking any immediate risk, but there's no real reward in terms of the growth of your principal either. So the goal should be to move out on the risk/reward continuum in tandem, in measured steps. You don't want to dive into the deep end of a swimming pool for returns if it means assuming a Pacific Ocean full of risk.

In practice, the best way to get an appropriate reward for the chance you're taking is to hold an extremely diversified investment portfolio. This delivers the returns of an entire market in exchange for assuming its risks. The easiest way to do this is through buying low-expense, tax-efficient index funds wherever possible. Unless you're some kind of investment genius, you don't want to make specialized bets on the game. You want to own the whole board.

How to Invest

There are several investment goals in this decade of your life, including establishing retirement accounts, setting aside emergency funds, and preparing for major life events such as buying a house. We'll look at these one by one.

Retirement

As paradoxical as it may seem, the first thing a 23-year-old employee needs to do is begin saving for retirement. This sounds crazy, since that time is many years away, but it happens to be the smart move. The money you put away now will have the power to compound tax-deferred, and the interest you earn on that interest will end up painlessly paying for your old age. Do yourself one of the biggest favors of your life and open a retirement account as early as possible.

While some companies still offer defined-benefit pension plans, saving for retirement these days usually means taking the maximum pretax deduction from your paycheck and stuffing the proceeds into your employer's 401(k) (or 403(b), for those in education and nonprofits) plan. If your company offers a partial match of your contribution, so much the better. Don't even think about leaving this money on the table. There aren't many $100 bills lying on the sidewalks of life; this is one of them. When you make your contributions happen automatically, they become a comparatively painless method of regular saving.

The quality of these 401(k)/403(b) plans varies widely. If you work for a big company, you're likely to have a plan with Vanguard, Fidelity, or the like, with excellent options for investing your money. Smaller companies will tend to have far more limited choices with higher expenses. These fees are typically buried in the fine print, because all too often neither the sponsoring fund company nor your company's human resources department wants you to see how much you're paying.

What if your job doesn't have a retirement plan? At a minimum, you can probably open a Roth IRA and salt away $4,000 a year. There may be other plans that fit you as well: Keoghs, SIMPLE, SEP IRAs, solo 401(k)s, or Roth 401(k)s. There's some talk about consolidating all these confusing plans, so be sure to check on what the current offerings are. The idea, though, is that they let your dollars compound unmolested by the IRS, and, in the Roth editions, with a promise to let you withdraw your money tax-free later as well.

But how should you invest the funds you're putting aside for retirement? What should your portfolio look like in today's world? Figure 4.1 shows an ideal asset allocation for someone in their 20s:

Figure 4.1: 20s Asset Allocation

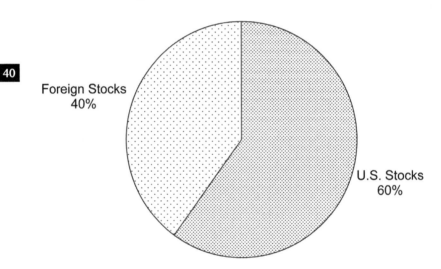

This plan, invested 100 percent in equities, is quite aggressive. We think that this is an acceptable risk, both because you'll have some time for diversification in your corner as you make these contributions over the course of a decade, and because you have the virtue of a long time horizon to smooth out any speed bumps you hit along the way.

Understand that your account will fluctuate wildly in value. Just stick this pie in the oven, keep the automatic deposits flowing, and don't worry about how much the account is worth for any given quarter. All that really matters is what its value will be on the day you retire.

Your authors love index funds. They're inexpensive and simply seek to replicate the performance of some broad market index of securities. The major finding of the past 30 years in finance is that these routinely beat the performance of higher-priced funds that employ active stock pickers in an attempt to beat the market. It turns out that the market as a whole seems to do an excellent job of processing most of the publicly available information about the prospects for various companies and incorporating this data into a stock's price.

On the other hand, active managers whose job is to find undervalued stocks (which then will presumably appreciate more than the rest) have a poor record when it comes to actually being able to do so. It's not that the marketplace is perfect in assigning prices; but that the mispricing that does occur (the over- and undervaluation of securities) tends to be random and quickly evaporates once discovered. The bitter truth is that investment strategies based on the premise of trying to beat the market don't work very well, especially after all the added expenses are taken into account.

41

Instead of "beating the market," we recommend *being* the market." The best strategy for most people is simply harvesting returns as cheaply and efficiently as possible. For the U.S. stock portion of your portfolio, we would look for a "Total Stock Market Index" or "S&P 500 Index" fund. These track broad market indexes such as the Wilshire 5000 Index, the Russell 3000 Index, the Morgan Stanley U.S. Broad Market Index, or the Standard & Poor's 500 indexes. These are lists of the largest stocks by market capitalization that trade on the domestic stock markets, with a few tweaks thrown in to determine eligibility for index membership. By purchasing these funds, you'll own a very small stake in the fortunes of most of the larger, publicly traded companies in the United States.

For the Foreign Stock portion, we would look for an "EAFE Index" or a "Total International Index" fund. These typically track the Morgan Stanley Europe, Australia, and Far East Index. Sometimes they throw in some representation of the Morgan Stanley

Emerging Markets Index as well. Since over half of the global economy is now located abroad, you'll want to have a substantial exposure to these markets. Most 401(k) plans have far fewer options for international investing than they do for the U.S. market, unfortunately.

If at all possible, pass on your own company's stock. The point is to diversify your risks away from your job, not concentrate them by putting all your eggs in the company basket.

If you can't decide which fund to choose from those presented on the palette, you can punch the fund's ticker symbol into **www. morningstar.com** to see how many stars it gets, or better still, just pick the one with the lowest expense ratio (since the more expensive the fund, the worse it usually performs). Perhaps you know someone who seems to have their head on straight as far as investing is concerned, who can advise you as to the best choices from your company's list of offerings. The guy or gal who works in the accounting office is often a better person to ask than the flashy salesman who's always bragging about his latest stock picks at the watercooler.

42

Cash Reserves

After your retirement saving is set up and on autopilot, the next thing you need is some cash to cover any contingencies that arise above and beyond the day-to-day items in your budget. What if your car breaks down and needs $500 worth of repairs? What if you get laid off and need to tide yourself over for a month while you find a new job? What if your dad gets sick and you need to make an unexpected trip back to Akron to visit him? Bad things happen to good people, and good people have to be prepared to pay for them.

The best place to store some money like this is in a money market fund. Lots of places will offer high teaser rates, but Vanguard offers many that are the best of breed. ING Direct and Emigrant Direct are two Web-based operators who will link their high-interest money market fund directly to your checking account, allowing you to make electronic transfers between the two online (you can find links to these on the Stein-DeMuth Website).

By way of comparison, the so-called money market fund at your local bank often pays a poor rate of interest, so don't let its name fool you. Find the fattest yield you can for your emergency fund—and don't put it into a CD. The whole point is that you have to be able to get your hands on this money when you least expect to need it.

In general, your authors aren't big believers in keeping huge amounts in cash reserve accounts. The reason is the low returns that these pay in exchange for their stable $1 net asset value and instant access. Typically, your money's return will lag behind inflation. As our financial-advisor friend Ray Lucia puts it, dollars in the bank are like hamburgers on a grill: They just sit there shrinking (because they're affected by the fire of inflation). There's also the psychology to consider: If your money is just loafing around in such an account, you'll be very tempted to spend it on items that aren't the kind of legitimate uses for which it was intended.

43

A few thousand dollars ought to be enough to cover the kinds of emergencies that most 20-year-olds are likely to face. If you have a solid job with a big company, you can probably get by with having enough cash in your reserve fund to cover about two months' worth of expenses. If you're self-employed and looking at a highly variable income stream, you might want as much as four to six months' worth of income on tap.

Investment Accounts

The typical twentysomething won't have great sums to invest after setting aside money for retirement, cash reserves, and all your other budget items. But if you do, we'll give you a peek into a crystal ball: You have two big, hairy expenses coming up within the next decade:

1. House
2. Kids

The sooner you can start saving for them, the better off you'll be. Your next move is to open an investment account somewhere cheap: Vanguard, Fidelity, T. Rowe Price, E*trade, or the like.

How should you invest this money? You can't sink it all in the stock market, because if the market corrects at exactly the point when you need the funds, you're in trouble. These expenses may hit you at any point in the next decade, so you need to be correspondingly prudent with your investment decision here. You could keep it in cash or short-term bonds, but these don't offer you much in the way of prospects for growth.

We think the best compromise is to use something called a "balanced" mutual fund, which combines stocks, bonds, and cash in a judicious mixture. The hope is that this will be a "Goldilocks" fund—not too hot, not too cold—which will give you a better return than cash but less volatility than stocks. Unless you work in finance or have made a great study of investing, there's no reason to complicate this process. Table 4.1 lists some single, balanced funds to consider for one-stop shopping, depending on where you want to open your account. They're listed in order of their ascending expense ratios. (Note that any one of these funds should serve your purpose; you don't need all four.)

Table 4.1: Balanced Funds

Sponsor	Fund	Ticker	% Stock	% Bonds	% Cash	Expense
Vanguard	Lifestrategy Conservative Growth	VSCGX	45%	46%	9%	0.25%
Fidelity	Fidelity Asset Manager	FASMX	41%	29%	22%	0.73%
T Rowe Price	TRP Personal Strategy - Income	PRSIX	47%	40%	14%	0.80%
Schwab	Schwab MarketTrack Conservative	SWCGX	40%	46%	7%	0.91%

These funds all offer a conservative mix of stocks, bonds, and cash. Their value will go up and down with the markets, but you aren't trying to shoot the moon (as you are with your retirement allocation at this point), and you're not giving up on growth entirely (as you are with your cash reserves). The account should grow over time, and the money should be there when you need it. These funds aren't perfect, but they have the enormous advantage of simplicity.

One caveat: Once you actively start looking for a house, take the amount you need for the down payment out of this account immediately and put it into your cash reserves. You can't afford to take any risks with that portion of your money at that point.

◆

Amazingly, **Yodlee.com** will let you display all the balances from all your different bank, brokerage, 401(k), and credit-card accounts on a single "dashboard" that you can access online. You just enter your account numbers and passwords at Yodlee's OnCenter, and they'll do the rest for free. They'll even keep track of your frequent flier miles. You'll find a link on the Stein-DeMuth Website.

You've now laid the foundation for investing that will serve you well for the rest of your life. What about all your friends who brag about how well they're doing with their hot stocks? Ignore them. They'll be punished eventually.

By following these simple precepts, your investments will do better than those of the vast majority of investors, and you'll be on the right trajectory to meet the upcoming obligations of your financial life.

45

▰▰▰

CHAPTER 5

SINGLES

In 2004, the Census Bureau tells us, there were over five million Americans between the ages of 20 and 34 who were living alone. Single people have their own set of financial challenges and opportunities.

We've seen that in the first decade on the job there's a steep increase in inflation-adjusted wages for most young Americans. This is because the new employee gradually learns to do more and better work, much like software that's brought out in better, more advanced versions each year. Just as companies would pay a higher price for the upgraded functionality of improved software, they'll shell out more for the better worker.

At the same time, it's quite—in fact, more than quite—possible for the new worker to spend every bit of his salary and, with the aid of credit cards, far more still. The temptation to expand consumption faster than income is even more pressing for the young and fabulous than for the married and square. After all, the latter can see that they have responsibilities to each other and to their progeny, but singles see their responsibilities as being primarily to themselves.

Further, married couples tend to consider a longer time horizon in their spending decisions. Singles see their status as both more uncertain and also requiring less planning, since fewer people's lives are involved. If things don't work out, perhaps they can marry some rich person who will give them a fresh start.

We don't want to stereotype here. Not every single person is a swinging guy or girl just waiting to spend that paycheck at Hedonism II in Jamaica. There are many extremely sensible single men and women in this country who want to be sure that, whatever the future holds, they're prepared with ample savings. But it's well known to social scientists that married Americans accumulate far more savings than do singles. Whether because of hypnotic sales pitches or the insecurities of single life (or the ecstasy of single life or the torture of single life), as a group, these individuals tend to get themselves into financial trouble more often, and are three to four times more likely to end up declaring bankruptcy than are their married counterparts.

One of your authors (Phil DeMuth) recalls the case of a psychotherapy patient he once knew. This beautiful young woman was married, employed, and the model of financial probity, always paying her therapist in a timely manner. However, her husband was inattentive. Marital counselors were consulted, and it was determined that this marriage Could Not Be Saved. Divorce followed, and within a few short months, this woman was out every night doing tequila shots and exploring the advanced chapters of the *Kama Sutra*. It wasn't long before she lost her job and fell into arrears on her therapy bill.

Thus, by the time young single Americans reach "square two," that square is often stamped in red ink with "Past Due."

What Happened to Rhett Butler?

The single woman in America is by no means certain to get married. This is basically because the allure of marriage for both men and women has diminished so drastically in the last 35 years that the percentage of Americans who remain single has doubled, and for some age and gender subgroups, tripled.

The woman who's 29, spending every penny she earns while waiting for P. Charming to come along and set her financial house in order with his huge inheritance, shouldn't count on it quite as firmly as she might have in, say, 1958. (The number of single young men with the resources to bail out their fiancées isn't large, and this imagined man might not come along at all. Even if he does, she may not like him.) All of this means that she needs to rely mainly upon herself for rescue from fiscal catastrophe.

In addition, the future needs of both single men and women may be even more pressing than those of married people, even if there's no child forthcoming. This is because the income expectations of singles aren't as rosy as those of married people, for a variety of reasons. This is the bad news.

Income tends to rise largely because of increased productivity, which, on an individual basis, tends to be highly correlated with longevity on the job. Employers pay more to employees who have been with the company longer.

This is a problem for the young and the restless, who tend to stay with companies for shorter periods and change positions more frequently than do the married. In the first decade of work, the difference is less pronounced than in later years. But as time goes by, those differences add up and become quite significant.

The income trend lines of the single don't rise as fast as those of the married for yet another reason: The latter tend to be promoted and paid as if they had greater needs and more reliability. In other words, they tend to earn more just by virtue of being married. Of course, this is illegal per se under federal law. But regardless of what the statutes say, when salary committees meet, they take into account whether or not an employee has a wife and babies at home who need to be fed.

We describe the world as it operates, not some ideal that we might wish could be. Survey data have shown time after time that businesses pay more when they know that a man or woman has a family to support. Also, when salaries and promotions are considered, married employees often look more solid than those who are single. Every employer, even in Hollywood and even in the music business, likes a reliable worker. The married person often gets a promotion or a bigger paycheck simply due to the perception that the "family man" is a steady, hardworking guy.

Traps and Pitfalls

On the consumption side, expenses per person can often be greater for a single worker than for someone who's married. Mainly, this is because of the economies of scale associated with two people living together. While two can't live as cheaply as one, they can and do generally live as cheaply as 1.7. One person, on the other hand, can only live as cheaply as one.

Rent for two persons is often no more than for one, since most leases in this country are based on the size of the dwelling rather than on the number of occupants. While a husband and wife can split that expense, lowering the cost for each individual, the single man or woman must pay it all him- or herself. Housing expenses per person are higher for young single men and women than for any other group.

Another increased cost for singles is automobile insurance. For many people just starting out in life, this is more expensive than the car payments themselves. It isn't uncommon for young Americans to spend more on car insurance than food. While this may be a remote concern for the carless Manhattanite, it's a matter of life or death for the suburbanite in Dallas or Denver. If this single person happens to own a convertible or a sports car, that expense quickly becomes prohibitive.

As bad as these problems are on both the income and consumption side, they can be dwarfed by the pressures of trying to keep up with all the fine young Joneses. A life filled with promotions can be thrown into pandemonium if you run with a crowd that has more money than you do. If you, a junior accountant at Macy's, find yourself among the heirs to Macy's, you may find that you have to go to Saint Bart's and Aspen each winter, buy a suit each month at Ralph Lauren, and generally live like a young merchant prince. The most well-constructed hopes and dreams for a solvent future are doomed before such an onslaught of showing off. If truth be told—and quite contrary to popular opinion—there's rarely great advantage to be gained from hanging around the rich. They'll mostly want to know what you can do for them for free.

Why Me?

You may well ask, "Why do I need substantial savings? Why shouldn't I have just enough to tide me over in case I want to give my boss the finger and look for another job? After all, I don't have to think about putting Junior and Sis through college, do I? I don't have to worry if they foreclose on my house, because I don't have one."

Part of the answer is that someday you probably *will* have a little Junior to feed and clothe and put through school. But before we get to that part of the drama, look at what having some savings can mean to a young single person.

If being single means having a degree of independence that married people don't, consider that savings mean *real* freedom. Even if you're a single guy with ten girlfriends (a crime that would be its own punishment), you aren't free if you have a Visa bill that's ten times your monthly wage. Even if you're a single woman who'd never consider being tied down in order to send hubby through med school, never dream of devoting your life to changing diapers and being chained to the PTA, you're thoroughly and completely enslaved if you have to stay at your job, in your current apartment, in the same town, all in the name of reducing your bill at Neiman Marcus.

To be really free in modern society (and maybe in old society, too) means having some measure of financial independence. Being a free spirit is meaningless if you're deeply in debt. If being single means sleepless nights wondering how those bills are ever going to be paid and if anyone will ever be around to share the burdens, then insolvency and looming financial catastrophes are a dead weight you don't need.

According to Three Dog Night, one is the loneliest number. For many people, it's frightening to be alone. Even those who spend the evenings at the local hot club, drinking Cosmos until daybreak, often wake up wondering if there will be anyone to care for them if something tragic happens. One of the best sleeping pills is the knowledge that you're taking good care of yourself and that if something doesn't go as planned, you'll be all right. If you know that you're financially prepared and can save a little bit month by month, you'll be able to pass through those dead-of-night crises far better than if you have a radioactive American Express bill glowing on the nightstand. If you've kept your consumption of clothes, cars, and vacations low enough so that you won't feel your mouth go dry if you don't get that anticipated raise, you're ahead of the game.

Notches on Your Belt

How do you do that? How do you set yourself apart from the generality of young people and get yourself into a position of financial strength? First and foremost, spend less.

There are several areas in which single people tend to overspend. We've already covered the "show-off" category, which an economist might call "recreation expenses not otherwise classified": travel, clothing, restaurants, and bars. These line items are so obviously either under control or not that they scarcely require further discussion. The big-ticket items are even more important.

52

Your Car

Many young single people spend unwisely on automobiles. These expenses tend to be significantly higher per person for single people than for those in the same age-group who are married. This category tends to be additive as well: If you fork over a lot of money for a used Jaguar, you're also likely to spend a lot repairing, insuring, and maintaining it. If you purchase an entry-level Mercedes, you're going to find that taking the dings out of the door panels costs a small fortune.

Making a hard-and-fast rule for how much to spend in this category is impossible, because a car means much more to some people than to others. A rule such as "one week's pay for all automobile expenses" is both far too lavish for people who are indifferent to what they drive and perhaps too modest for those who absolutely love cars. But if you find yourself spending more than 25 percent of your take-home pay on a car, that machine should make you happier than your boy- or girlfriend. If you're spending more on your car than on your housing, your car is probably a passion like heli-skiing that you can't really afford at this point in your life.

To whatever extent you can substitute the peace of mind of having savings for the mad ecstasy and terror of owning a Corvette, you'll come out ahead. As you make do with your own charm and lovable nature rather than showing up in a gleaming new black Mustang, you're getting ahead in other ways. The young man or woman who can achieve status within his or her group without having to overspend on a car is far better off than those who rely on major expenditures for steel, chrome, glass, and rubber to make themselves feel important.

There are several Web resources for car buyers. Motley Fool will talk you out of buying a car, the annual auto issue of *Consumer Reports* will tell you about the most reliable used-car bets, and **Edmunds.com** will show you the total cost of ownership over five years (which often varies significantly among competing models). The smart move is generally to buy a lightly used Japanese car and then not replace it until the engine falls out. This strategy can make a surprisingly large difference to your lifetime net worth, especially as compared with that of the person who leases a new car every two or three years.

But for all the issues of automobiles and speed, the biggest area of possible savings for single people has to be in their biggest cost: housing.

Your Home

People who live alone tend to have a preference for it. Generally speaking, they know that it's much more expensive than living with someone else. Many young single people have had roommates (or a succession of roommates) and now are sick and tired of having to worry about somebody else's dirty socks or unwashed dishes, along with the countless psychodramas that come with them. Those who live alone have had it with phone calls at midnight from roommates' former boy- or girlfriends who want one more chance. Someone shelling out half of her salary or his wages for single living quarters knows all too well the pain of splitting gas bills and Christmas gifts to the trash collectors. The man or woman living alone has decided that the cost of living solo is worth every penny.

This is all well and good, but this kind of young person should realize that every other expense must be scrutinized with an electron microscope to get over the financial hurdle of that solo-apartment rental bill. It's completely understandable that human beings should want peace and quiet where they live. Nevertheless, if they don't make serious adjustments in other costs, this will make it difficult to keep their financial lives on track.

Specifically, this means paying careful attention to clothing, meals away from home, travel, gifts (for some reason, this is a huge expense item for singles), Blackberries, and G4 Powerbooks. It also means that the single person would be doing him- or herself a huge financial favor by managing to somehow find a companionable roommate. The cost per person of sharing a two-bedroom apartment is generally lower than the cost of two studios. This arrangement also reduces the cost of utilities, often cuts down on meals eaten away from home, and can also lower recreation costs. After all, it's sometimes more fun to watch *Seinfeld* reruns with your roomie than to go out to a movie. If you can stand living with someone else, it will be much easier to keep your expenses under control.

If you can't bear even to think about a roommate, then you must go back to shaving expenses elsewhere . . . or you could earn more money.

Navigating Around the Averages

There's no commandment saying that men and women aren't allowed to work at more than one job or to take classes that raise their earnings. If this is true for married couples—and it is—it's true in No Trump for those on their own.

The single man or woman can't send a clone to work, but he or she can get another job. Fewer and fewer young people are doing hard physical labor in the mines or fields by day, so they aren't dead tired when they come home from work. In fact, there are many who are so bored by their nine-to-five jobs that they're dying to get out and do something different in the evening. If they can get paid for it, more power to them.

If your expenses tend to outstrip your income, you can cut your expenses, or you can seek to raise your income (or both). It may well turn out that you get more pleasure—as well as income—out of teaching a night-school class than you would out of eating at home more often. You may meet more friends by working at Circuit City than staying at home talking to your mother on the telephone.

Another avenue more open to the single than to the married person is to raise her productivity, and hence her pay. The married man or woman inherently has something to do each evening and on weekends; the single person by definition doesn't. He or she is free to take courses in computer science, transmission repair, or new strategies for trusts and estate planning or to finish that MBA. Those courses lead to new jobs and promotions. Part-time schooling is one of the all-time best ways for a single person to increase income—even more than taking a second job—because the new skills raise your productivity in your primary job and across your entire working life. Go back and examine Figure 2.1 (page 13), and you'll see the advantage that further education can confer.

55

While there are averages and generalities about income and various groups, what you take home is largely determined by your own exertions. The average man or woman in his or her 20s may see what they make nearly double in the decade. But there are those whose income will triple because they learned more, worked harder, or made better connections. Others will have their earnings rise by much less, because they did not work, did not learn, or did not make contacts.

Add It Up

In summary: As a young single man or woman, you have the chance to take advantage of a steep upward curve in your income. The key is to:

- Greatly restrain your consumption of certain items such as travel, restaurant meals, bar tabs, clothing, entertainment, and most especially automobiles.

- Try to get some handle on your housing expenses, which will tend to be far higher for you as a single than for married people (per person).

- If you don't get a handle on housing costs, you must adjust all other expenses correspondingly.

In a word, young singles have a great opportunity to fortify their economic position because of typically high earnings growth combined with low real need for basic expenses. Take advantage of it.

◢◥◢

CHAPTER 6

Housing for Married Couples and Singles

The biggest purchase most of us will ever make in our lives is our residence. Figure 6.1 shows the average price of a house in the United States since 1963, according to Census Bureau data:

Figure 6.1: Average U.S. House Price 1963–2004

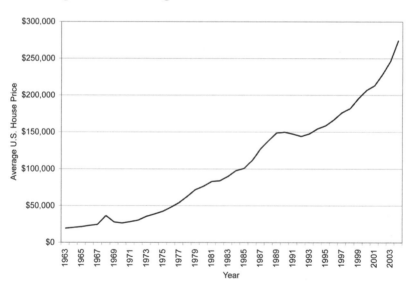

Notice the direction in which housing prices have been going: up. In 2004, the average price for a house was $274,500. In many parts of the country, owning a home has gotten to be more expensive than anyone would have even imagined a few years ago. Whether you call it a "boom" or a "bubble," even if home prices drop 20 percent from here, they'll still be expensive compared to yesterday.

How can anyone afford to buy? To understand what's going on behind these figures, we need to look at the data more closely.

To begin with, there's something misleading about referring to *average* housing prices. To get an average, you lump all the prices together and divide by the number of homes. But these figures are skewed upward. A house can't cost less than nothing, but at the other end of the spectrum, there's no upper limit. It's difficult to imagine even a plywood shack costing less than $10,000 these days, while Bill Gates's home might cost $50 million. Add these two together and you get an average price of $25,007,500. Lots of people have built McMansions over the past decade, and all of these push the average price of a house to a misleadingly high level.

For this reason, it's better to look at the *median:* Half the houses are more expensive than this price, and half are less; it's the 50th percentile. This isn't artificially inflated by movie-star homes in Malibu. By this standard, the median price for a house was $221,000 in 2004. This is still extremely high—we are, after all, at the end of a boom or a bubble—but at least it's down from the stratosphere.

The median price of a house in the U.S. has appreciated 6.3 percent annually on average since 1963, but even this overstates the investment value of a home. If you subtract inflation, this drops to an average increase of 1.6 percent per year. Also consider that the median house in 2004 is much bigger and much nicer than the median house of 1963. Our friend Professor Robert Shiller of Yale University has tried to control for this factor by compiling an index that looks at same-house resales over time. His conclusion? Historically, home prices are flat after inflation.

The primary benefit home buyers receive may not stem from the rise in their residence's inflation-adjusted price, but from the value of the imputed rent: the fact that home owners are essentially writing the rent check to themselves and aren't being taxed on this income (as they are in some other countries). This isn't to say that some places haven't appreciated more than others, and more at some times than others. Housing markets are local: Some areas (New York, Florida, and California) have a boom-and-bust speculative cycle, while most other regions just slowly chug along. Prices vary widely across the country.

Now, you *could* get ahead by moving to an area that has inexpensive housing prices. The problem is that these also tend to be areas where the prospects for high-paying jobs are circumscribed as well. You might get a great deal on a house in Radioactivity, Utah, but if the only job within 500 miles is operating the Slurpee machine at the gas station by the interstate, you're not really that much ahead of the game on a net basis.

Conversely, the areas with the super-expensive homes tend to be places with high-paying jobs for people with desirable skills. The main exception at the pricy end of the market would be places like the Hamptons or Aspen, where rich people keep their second homes. Here, the housing is astronomically expensive, and at the same time, there's little high-paying work. The locals eventually can't afford to live there, so help must be bused in. Areas like these offer ordinary middle-class home buyers the worst of both worlds (but they are pretty).

Much is made of the home owner's ability to access one of the few remaining legal tax shelters available to ordinary Americans, although capping this deduction has recently been contemplated by the Bush tax team. Still, we wouldn't count on it changing anytime soon. The tax benefit involved in buying a home with borrowed money is basically that the interest on your mortgage is deductible from your income for purposes of computing state and federal income tax liability (as is the property tax). In the first few years of a mortgage, almost all the payments are for interest and very little for reducing principal. In turn, this means that almost all of your checks to the mortgage company will be deductible from your income for tax purposes.

Let's say that you bought a median-priced home for $221,000. Of course, remember that you don't have to do so—by definition, half of the homes sold cost less than this. Furthermore, since it will be extremely difficult to come up with the standard, ultra-desirable 20 percent down payment of $44,200 without getting an inheritance from your rich Aunt Lily, let's say that you can cough up $22,000, or about 10 percent down from your own efforts. This means that you'll have to buy private mortgage insurance and pay a higher rate of interest, but so be it. At today's rates (currently 6.5 percent), your mortgage costs will come to about $15,288 a year for 30 years. The interest portion of that $15,288 comes to $12,870 for the first year and is deductible from your taxable income on Schedule A of Form 1040. Not bad. Except that the *standard* deduction available to joint filers who don't itemize deductions is already $10,000. Unless you have a lot of other deductions to claim, the advantage of the mortgage isn't overwhelming. After 14 years, you're actually better off forgoing the mortgage-interest deduction and taking the standard deduction instead.

For the median American home buyer, there can be less to the value of the mortgage tax deduction than meets the eye, but don't count on your Realtor or mortgage broker pointing this out to you. In fact, you should be aware that everyone you consult in the process of buying a home has a vested interest in selling you the house as quickly and at as high a price as possible.

Let us hasten to add the rest of the negatives of home ownership: Houses are relatively illiquid, which means that they're difficult to sell quickly for full market price. Transaction costs for the sale are high, perhaps 10 percent total, not the least of which is the 6 percent that you'll have to pay the Realtors. Then there are property taxes, maintenance costs, and homeowner's insurance. There's also an invisible expense (known as *opportunity cost*): The money you put into the down payment might be more profitably invested elsewhere, such as the stock market. But in spite of the fact that the benefits of home ownership can be oversold, we're still wild about the idea of your buying your own home—if you can afford it.

Reasons to Buy a Home

In most areas, most of the time it will be cheaper to buy than to rent over the long run, even allowing for the fact that the renter gets to put his down payment in the stock market. If you hold on to your house for a number of years, it will likely appreciate beyond the various transaction costs of selling, and you'll discover that you've lived essentially rent free. (The exception to the buying-beats-renting rule would be if you were to buy into a red-hot real-estate market near the top. If the market subsequently corrects 40 percent, you'll be waiting a long time to recoup your investment, and wishing the whole time that you'd rented instead.)

Many of the benefits of home ownership are psychological. First among these comes the sense of peace you have in knowing that nothing short of a bank foreclosure or a government eviction can get you out of your space. Feeling "grounded" is more than just a play on words.

When you own your home, if you want to paint a room black, you can go ahead and do so if you feel like it (although we don't recommend it). Your mortgage payment actually gets a little smaller each month because it's being eaten away by inflation, while your house's price generally increases in lockstep with inflation, if not more. This point bears repeating: *Inflation acts on your mortgage, but not on your home's value.* By the time you retire, you may well own your home outright, and if you're like most people, it will be your single largest asset.

Home owners are savers. There's something in their temperament that leads them to accumulate assets in a way that renters just plain don't. According to the AARP, in 2001 home owners had $175,000 in net worth ($91,000 in other assets besides their homes), compared to a total net worth of only $7,000 for renters. This difference isn't explained by any of the usual demographics, but it's not hard to understand why it exists.

Once bought with a mortgage, a house, condo, townhome, or co-op requires that payments be made on a monthly basis. Otherwise, a legal penalty is incurred. The mortgage will fall into default and the home will be sold by the lender if checks aren't received in a regular and timely fashion. This means that the young couple's payments for the home aren't only a form of saving; more than that, they're a form of *enforced* saving. The couple is simply not allowed to stop saving in this fashion without facing severe penalties and complications to their lives.

However conscientious a young couple may be, using whatever plan for savings they may have drawn up with the very best of intentions, they'll still be tempted to go off the wagon from time to time. The lure of taking a break from a savings program is enormous. There's always some good reason—a sale at a department store, for example—to postpone putting money aside. If you rely solely on your own discretion to keep on track, you may succeed and you may not. You'll have to renew your commitment every time you walk by a store window. But when your saving is enforced by law and contract, with the underlying penalty of losing your home, you'll discover that you're far more regular in this habit.

A home bought with a mortgage is, to that extent, a leveraged asset. A primary residence is bought with mostly borrowed money. That amount, called a mortgage, has generally been available at interest rates that are lower than the annual increase in the value of your house. *For the price of the down payment plus the monthly payment, you participate in the housing market at the full price of your home.*

To oversimplify: If your $100,000 home appreciates 3 percent in one year, it's then worth $103,000. But if you only put down $10,000, you've made $3,000 on your initial outlay, for a return of 30 percent. Your savings have been added to by the leverage involved in buying a dwelling. In other words, you're making money with other people's money. You not only save by putting cash into your house each month, you'll also earn on the savings of the bank or savings and loan depositors which have been lent to you for your mortgage. In that miraculous way, you'll get the benefit of both your own saving and that of total strangers.

In addition, when you own a home, you're effectively both your own landlord and tenant. This means that you get to pocket the value of the rent that your home could otherwise claim if you, as landlord, were to lease it to someone else. Were you to rent a $100,000 residence, that might cost you $5,000 a year. Since you're the owner, however, you forgo this expenditure.

Of course, there are dangers. Should you buy a home in the midst of a falling market, you'll find that your savings are locked up in a trap of illiquidity and loss. But even so, things will eventually turn again, this time in your favor. For this reason, your home is best considered a long-term investment, and enforced saving by this method has been an extraordinarily good way for young people to save and invest. By happy coincidence, these are the same habits that allow one to make good long-term preparation for having and raising children.

How Much Should You Spend?

There's an old-fashioned rule that has some relevance even today: The monthly cost of paying for a house shouldn't be much higher than the cost of renting it would be, if you also include the tax savings from the mortgage interest. Real estate agents sneer at this homely adage and say that the reason you should be happy to pay four times as much in monthly mortgage payments as you would to rent is that you're going to make so much money when you sell.

That can be true or false. When you buy a house and pay for it over 30 years, any excess you shell out over the monthly rental cost is in fact a wager that your home will rise in value faster than the interest rate on that money would raise its value. If you pay a high price for a house, that amount includes something for living there and something as a bet that the property's worth will increase.

People in their 20s and 30s (or any other age) should always be wary about the premium they pay for that bet on future appreciation. If the price is far above the rental value of the house, then caution is in order.

One Scenario

We plugged a home purchasing scenario into our monster lifetime income- and consumption-smoothing software, ESPlanner, to see what insight it might shed on the process. Let's walk through this in some detail, because we're going to be exploring some similar scenarios later.

63

We assumed that the home buyers were a married couple. Highlights include:

- They just turned 31, and they know that they want to buy a house.

- Both work full-time and earn a median income for 31-year-olds: he = $38,000, she = $31,000.

- They already have some money in their retirement plans: he = $20,000, she = $10,000.

- They plan to retire when they turn 66 and then live until they're 92, when, for our convenience, they'll die on schedule.

- Social Security benefits will be cruelly cut by 25 percent on the day they retire.

What's the best course of action for this couple, given their goals and assuming that they'd like their lifestyle to have as smooth a ride as possible on their way to the promised land?

The answer is that they both need to immediately start saving for a down payment. In order to get their hands on this money, they probably need to suspend making contributions into their retirement accounts for several years. This sounds like financial-planning heresy but is actually prudent. The precise form that savings take isn't as important as the fact of the saving itself. If they were taking the money that was supposed to go into their 401(k) plans and blowing it on trips to Portofino, that would be another story.

A house, however, is an appreciating asset with its own set of tax benefits, and one that holds out the tantalizing prospect of rent-free living. Furthermore, once purchased, it enforces future savings for many years to come. This is a great investment for them. Under these circumstances, it's perfectly valid to take money that otherwise would go into their retirement plans and divert it to a different asset class. If push comes to shove, they can always take out a reverse mortgage against their house and use it to supplement their retirement income later. Naturally, it would be far better both to continue their retirement contributions and save for the down payment. Our goal here is to get them into a house.

Figure 6.2 shows the basic pattern of saving and spending required for this couple to maintain their lifestyle on an even keel. It describes the "savings-management" program of withdrawals and deposits into and out of the savings accounts that buffer their financial lives. On the horizontal axis is their age (they're both the same age). On the vertical axis is the amount of money that they should add to their savings (positive numbers) or withdraw from their savings (negative numbers) each year in order to maintain their overall lifestyle at the same level over time. Each year's level of saving or withdrawal is marked by a little triangle on the graph.

Figure 6.2: Recommended Annual Contributions to or Withdrawals from Savings for Median-Income Family to Maintain an Even Lifestyle when Buying a House

65

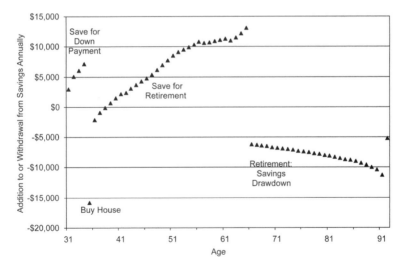

Here's how it works:

- From ages 31 to 34, they save progressively larger amounts ranging from $3,000 to $7,000 annually into a "house down payment" fund. They keep this in one of the balanced funds shown in Table 4.1 (on page 44). But as soon as they start actively looking for a house, they put their down payment into a money market fund to guard against loss.

- Then in the fifth year, at age 35, they dip into their savings for a 10 percent down payment on a median-priced house, taking out a 30-year mortgage at market rates, and continue drawing from these savings for the next few years thereafter.

- At age 39, they return to saving once more, this time into their retirement accounts at work, putting away larger amounts each year in pace with their rising incomes, right up until they retire at age 66.

- Because they bought the home with a 30-year mortgage when they turned 36, it was exactly paid off on the day they retired. This was careful planning.

- After retiring, they begin drawing down their retirement accounts, leaving them with exactly nothing in the bank on the day they both die. However, their house is completely paid off. Should either of them live longer, it could always be used as the source of a reverse mortgage, or sold outright to fund further living expenses. If one of them were to die before age 92, the survivor would have a nice little bump in income. (While we don't like to focus on this aspect of the equation, it's a potential angle for murder-mystery writers.)

Let's pause for a moment and consider another assumption we've made in the example above: the 10 percent down payment. This is a concession to the high price of housing today. It's far, far better to put down the conventional 20 percent, because then you're able to omit paying the dreaded private mortgage insurance.

Lenders know that people who put down less than 20 percent are far more likely to default on their loans. If the real estate market turns against them and they're "upside down" in their loans with a mortgage that's greater than the value of the house, these buyers will be very tempted to toss the keys back to the lender and just walk away, leaving someone else with the problem.

To prevent this eventuality, lenders require these home buyers to pool their risk by buying private mortgage insurance. For the couple in the example above, this will cost them more than $1,000 a year all by itself. They—and you—will be better off putting down 20 percent.

By saving and spending with the perfectly engineered precision of Figure 6.2, this couple was able to completely smooth out their average annual standard of living (defined here as the money available for current consumption after paying for housing expenses, taxes, and retirement savings) throughout their entire adult lives at $43,582 a year. While their expenditures and what they put aside (for their house and for their retirement) vary with each passing year, the amount they have available for current consumption for everything else remains constant.

In practice, no one is likely to do this; we're just using ESPlanner to highlight a strategy. We've already seen that Step 1 of getting a financial life is to acquire as much education and human capital as you can, and Step 2 is to start saving for retirement in your 20s. Step 3 is to save for a down payment for a home in your early 30s so that you can buy a house by the time you're in your mid-30s.

Saving and Spending Over the Life Cycle

If this couple wanted a more luxurious retirement, they could decide to save more now. Saving and consumption are on a seesaw. Spend more today and they have less to consume tomorrow; save more now and they have more to consume later. While this seems obvious, what isn't apparent is that the fulcrum isn't placed in the middle of the seesaw. *Saving a little more early on gives you the leverage to be able to spend much more later. Spending more when you're younger carries a high price tag that you pay when you're older, because it robs your savings of the power of long-term compounding.* It's easy to spend too much when we're young because the size of the dent it makes in our bank balance later is completely invisible until we get there and find the cupboard bare.

How does this impact the young home buyers we've just discussed? Put starkly, if they could live on $38,500 a year through their 30s and 40s (after housing, taxes, and retirement savings) instead of the $43,500 allotted to them in the example above, they could have $80,000 to live on every year after they retire instead of the $43,500 lifestyle they're currently slated to continue. The dollars saved now pay big dividends later. On the other hand, if they run up expenditures today, the possibility of financial trouble escalates after they're retired and have considerably fewer options for earning new money.

Housing for Singles: To Own or Not to Own

Should young single men and women buy homes if they have the savings for a down payment? Generally speaking, everyone who can afford to own should try to do so by the time they're in their mid-30s. The advantages are all to the home buyer in terms of reduced taxes, the certainty of future obligations (a fixed-rate mortgage has fixed payments, while rent can and does change at the whim of the landlord), the likelihood of price appreciation, the ability to use borrowed money to make money, and finally the freedom from the possible insanity of landlords. However, there is a trade-off. The renter has more money available for consumption today, but at the expense of less money tomorrow (relative to the home owner).

Even though buying a home is a good idea for most people at most times, there are definitely moments when doing so is similar to buying stock on October 20, 1929. No one can possibly know for certain when such times are. The only caution that must be borne in mind is that when the real estate agent tells you, "Yes, prices are high, but in five years all of this will seem like a bargain, and I guarantee you'll make money," that's often a very good time to run like heck. If the agent talks up some cleverly engineered mortgage product whereby you can live in the house for the first five years with only a one percent rate, this person is a tool of the devil.

More and more young single people are buying their own homes. During the housing boom, Americans of all ages and social conditions got the idea that they were fools for not doing so. Home ownership was considered the way to a prosperous future, and in fact, it is a good deal for most people. But two major factors make the answer less clear-cut for young singles; one consideration is demographic, and one is economic.

The demographic factor is that the great majority of single Americans between the ages of 20 and 29 will not be single by the time they're 39. It's unlikely that the single man in his 20s will remain that way for ten more years. When the wedding day comes, he may find that he wants to live in a different area from where he lived as a single. He may want to move from Greenwich Village to Riverdale, from Wrigleyville to Oak Park—in short, from city to suburb. But if he already owns a condo, he may find himself saddled with a home in the wrong neighborhood that's unsuitable for a married couple, and even less appropriate for a family with a baby.

By itself, that isn't a big problem. In a perfect world with a flawless free market, he could just sell that old dwelling to some new single and then take the profit and hightail it to suburbia. The problem is that the market is a long way from perfect. In real life, even in a lively market, houses take a long time to sell. In a weak resale environment, this can take an eternity. One of the most aggravating things in life is to have a house on the market for month after month, seeing hordes of lookie loos and not one buyer. Another maddening situation is to have almost all your assets tied up in bricks, mortar, landscaping, and chandeliers, which you can't turn into ready cash when you really need it.

This illiquidity (the inability to turn a real asset into cash at a fair market price) can be much more of a problem for a single person than for a family. After all, a family's housing arrangements are presumably set for some time to come, whereas those who are on their own can expect to get married and want a different home. That bachelor loft and bachelorette condo may have a lot of paper profit in them, but turning it into cash may turn out to be nearly impossible in the short run. Even if the market is humming, there will be high transaction expenses attendant upon selling your starter residence, which will eat away a considerable chunk of your profit.

The confluence of these two factors (likelihood of getting married plus the high cost of real estate transactions) can make buying a nightmare for a single man or woman. And the situation is often worse for the woman than it is for the man.

Unfortunately, there are many women in their 30s who have left work to get married, lost their seniority, gotten a new job, and then left it (with good reason) because it looked like a dead end, and therefore their incomes haven't risen as rapidly as might have been hoped. Likewise, there are many women (and men) with jobs that simply don't pay enough to allow for the purchase of a home, even though the individual's salary has been rising. There are also single women with dependent children who simply can't afford to buy, through no fault of their own. The real question is whether a single woman in her 30s should buy a house, knowing that paying for it will be a big struggle, in the hope and expectation that her income will rise enough in the future to make those payments manageable.

If you're in your 30s and contemplating buying a home, you should confidently expect to be able to grow into the payments if they're slightly out of reach at the date of closing. Your rising income will allow you to afford a far more valuable house in five years than you can now. It's great to have a home, wonderful to have a little plot of land with bricks and mortar that you can call your own. But of all the self-inflicted traumas of this world, few are more completely unnecessary and more readily avoided than making yourself "house poor." If this happens, you won't love your new place. Instead, it will be a millstone around your neck.

This means that the single woman in her 30s shouldn't assume that owning is so important a goal that it supersedes all others. In particular, it doesn't legitimize poverty and fear about every other area of her financial life. Owning a home is not the be-all and end-all of life. If the square peg won't fit into the round hole, she can reassure herself that there's more to life than holding title to a house.

The single woman should either make sure that she has an above-average income, or if she must buy a home, the property should be considerably less expensive than average. Otherwise, she's usually better off continuing to rent.

Single Buyers

There are some singles who, for whatever reason, feel quite certain that they'll never marry, or who have unshakable faith in their future in a certain part of town or even in a certain office or plant. For these people, buying a home makes sense. They'll get the tax benefits, the buildup of equity, and the security of owning their own dwelling without the heartache of suddenly having to move and being unable to sell.

While the argument about having more space for a baby may not apply, the arguments about compulsory saving apply even more forcefully to the single man or woman than to the married couple. Remember that single people tend to spend more and save less than those who have a spouse. Since a mortgage is a way of enforced saving, the single man or woman with a low probability of marrying, high job commitment, and a love of residential stability should strongly consider buying a home.

We ran the single life through our ESPlanner software to see what it counseled about buying versus renting. Figure 6.3 shows the projected course of lifetime consumption (spending money left after paying for housing and necessary savings) for two singles, one of whom buys a house at age 32, while the other continues to rent for the rest of his life. All the other variables are held constant. This illustrates the trade-offs.

Figure 6.3: Singles' Standard of Living: Renting vs. Buying a House

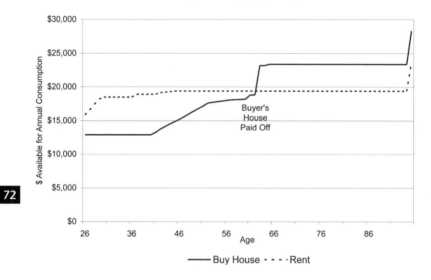

On the horizontal axis we see their ages. On the vertical axis, we see how much each of them gets to spend every year, after paying for their housing expenses, taxes, and retirement savings. The solid black line is the single who buys a house; the dotted black line is the single who's a lifelong renter.

Notice how the lines cross on the day the house is paid off. This isn't a coincidence. Up until this time, the renter has more money to spend because he's not slogging all that extra cash into his house payment and attendant expenses. But then the roles reverse: Suddenly the home owner has his house paid off and can redirect all the money he used to lavish on the mortgage into current consumption. The renter, on the other hand, has to keep writing that monthly check right up until the bitter end.

During their working lives, however, the single who rents has a 25 percent higher standard of living, on average. Since less of his money is tied up in his home, he has more to spend on his lifestyle—not an inconsiderable advantage for a single individual. By way of comparison, the home buyer has a richer retirement and dies leaving a house in his estate (as opposed to the renter, who, in this example, dies having successfully spent his last penny on himself).

Of course, many intermediate scenarios are possible. The home-buying single could decide to go with a less expensive home. The renter could choose to save more in his investment accounts and use it to fuel more consumption during retirement. Often, the decision between renting and owning comes down to how expensive a home is versus how high rent is. And for many people, the psychological predisposition to own or rent may outweigh the economic factors. After all, if either option were clearly more advantageous, almost everyone would choose it. The fact that both remain viable shows the general efficiency of the real estate marketplace.

73

The Home Buyer's Toolbox

A few nuts and bolts to consider with home ownership:

- Have your retirement account up and running before you start saving to buy a home.

- Save the money for the down payment in one of the funds we listed in Table 4.1 (see page 44) and put a padlock on it. Don't, under any circumstances, spend this money in some desperate attempt to placate a romantic prospect—past, present, or future.

- Don't buy a house in the middle of a market bubble in a bubble area, unless you know that you'll live there forever and you have sufficient cash flow to cover the mortgage in the event of a local real estate market meltdown. Rent and wait. There is an iron law of bubbles: They always stop.

- In case of fire, break glass: If you're truly disciplined and it's necessary to forgo your retirement savings to build up a down payment, then so be it. But this should be a last resort.

- Shop online for a mortgage. We're approaching the day when it will be a commodity that you can buy on price alone. Despite the best efforts of lenders to prevent this, by going online to Countrywide, E*trade, Eloan, Indymac Bank, Washington Mutual, and the like (there are links to all of these at **www.stein-demuth.com**), you can compare rates, points, closing costs, and so on. **Bankrate.com** also offers you a listing of the latest rates and purported best deals. What you find online is often better than the boutique rates that will be charged at your friendly neighborhood bank. The key thing is to compare the costs for all the different services involved so that you can make true like-to-like comparisons.

74

- Research "points." A point is one percent of the loan amount. By paying the lender more money now, up front, they'll offer you a lower interest rate on your mortgage in return, and hence a lower monthly payment going forward. Is it a good idea to pay points or not? This is a question with an empirical answer: It all comes down to how long you'll live in the home (which may be different from how long you *intend* to live there at the time you buy it). You can go to the Stein-DeMuth Website and find a link to a calculator to help you decide whether this makes sense.

- To get the best mortgage rate, have a good credit score. If you have a history of assuming debt and repaying it in a timely manner (as with a credit card and a car loan), the bank is happier to lend you money on more favorable terms than if you're an unknown factor or a bad risk.

- Decide on an adjustable versus a fixed rate. Because banks make money off their loan departments, they're very clever about engineering products that make it possible for you to assume much larger loans than is really prudent. Just because someone is willing to sell you a pack of cigarettes doesn't mean that you should take up smoking. Floating-rate loans frequently come with a "teaser" rate that's lower than what the payment will eventually be. There are zero-down payment, floating-interest loans with low teaser rates out there that are like ticking time bombs on the borrowers' balance sheets. No doubt there are situations under which these products work splendidly for all parties involved, but you won't be so lucky. Get a fixed-rate loan. If you can't afford one, you can't afford to buy the house.

- Do you want a 15- or 30-year mortgage? The former are much cheaper in the long run, saving you a fortune on interest. But at today's housing prices, the monthly payment may be out of reach. There's no shame in taking on a 30-year mortgage. Calculate it both ways and see if there's any way you can shorten it. There is also the much-ballyhooed option of taking on a 30-year mortgage and making extra payments to shorten the life of the loan, but we question how often people really send in that voluntary extra check.

- Remember that a mortgage is just the beginning: You'll also enjoy paying property tax. This is 1 to 3 percent of the home's price, with assessments varying dramatically across different areas.

- You'll need to insure your house, but you don't need to use the agency that your Realtor recommends. Ask friends and family members for references. You can also go online to **www.insure.com** or **www.insweb.com** and start your search there.

- If you've put down less than 20 percent, your lender will also require you to carry private mortgage insurance, which must be figured into the price.

- Total expenses of home ownership can add 40 percent annually to what you're paying on your mortgage. Your mileage may vary, of course.

- Make sure that the house you buy is one you can live in for a long, long time. It should see you through having children (the subject of our next chapter) and sending them to school. High transaction costs make changing your residence frequently an expensive, wealth-destroying proposition, unless you're a Realtor with an encyclopedic knowledge of the market.

- Plan to have the mortgage paid off by the time you retire. There may be valid exceptions to this rule, but they won't apply to you.

- Increasingly, online brokers are cracking the Realtors' lock on the market in some areas, offering partial rebates on commissions. It might pay to check out the likes of **redfin.com** and **ZipRealty.com**.

- Did anyone mention repairs and upkeep? "Home inspections" that are part of the buying process are typically extremely superficial (whether because of kickbacks or incompetence, we know not). If you can find an inspector who isn't in the pocket of the home-selling industry (maybe by using your brother-in-law, the general contractor?), you'll do better. But by far the best, most time-honored way to learn everything that's really wrong with a house is to buy it. You'll be amazed by what you discover. And it won't be a) pretty; b) anything like what you expected; or c) pretty, again.

CHAPTER 7

How to Have Babies

I f you thought buying a house was expensive, wait until you have children. There's a semifacetious basic rule about paying for children as they grow up: However much you think it will cost, it will be more. Within that maxim, there are several subrules:

- Whatever controls you try to put on your children's costs, they will not work.

- However much your neighbors can save on raising their kids, you won't be able to.

- Whatever you remember about the costs of growing up "back in the day," forget them.

The 2004 estimated total direct cost for a middle-income family to raise a child from the time he comes home with Mom from the hospital until he's 18 is $184,320. If you include all the indirect expenses (such as time lost from work, school taxes, prenatal health care—the whole enchilada, in other words), this figure grows to $242,070. Before you faint dead away, remember that you'll be spreading that cost over an 18-year period per child.

The cost of raising a child from just after birth to the beginning of higher education has been approximately 3.1 times one year's average income over the entire time period (for the first child). Children consume a disproportionately large amount for those with less income: about 5.1 times pretax earnings. Even though wealthier folks fork over nearly twice as much on their offspring as those with lower incomes do, they still get away with spending less as a total percentage of their income: about 2.6 times their average yearly draw spread out over the period.

When the first child comes along, consumption expenses rise (over time) by almost 25 percent. But by the time the third one comes down the pike, expenses rise by only about 7 percent. Rapidly diminishing costs greet each additional child as a general rule, which is good news.

Figure 7.1 shows how costs break down for typical child-raising American families at different income levels in 2004 dollars, courtesy of the U.S. Department of Agriculture.

Figure 7.1: Expenditures by Category on Children by Families at Different Income Levels

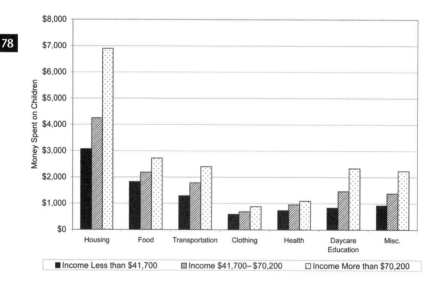

Figure 7.2 shows how these expenditures add up every year for one-, two-, and three-child families, depending on the families' income levels, also in 2004 dollars.

Figure 7.2: Total Expenditures on Children by Families at Different Income Levels by Number of Children

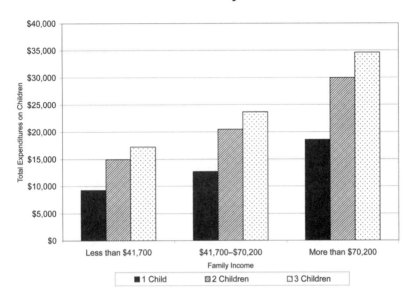

Shifting Budgets

When a couple in their 20s begins life today, they rarely do so in a large old house with a wide porch bequeathed to them by their maiden aunt. Instead, they enjoy wedded bliss in a tiny apartment with fiberboard walls and one bedroom leading into a living room with a couch and a color television set. When Baby comes along, that apartment is too small and must give way to a larger abode.

With only one infant child, the new dwelling may well be a two-bedroom apartment. But here's the rub: The average difference in cost between one- and two-bedroom apartments is extremely significant. If a median U.S. family moves from paying $553 per month for one bedroom to $650 for two, that's an increase in their housing costs of almost 20 percent.

If the family buys a freestanding home or rents a house as opposed to an apartment (possibly after the arrival of a second child), their out-of-pocket housing costs can rise by an even greater amount, often doubling or even tripling.

For example, if a family is paying $650 for an apartment and then decides that a house is a must, that median dwelling will cost $221,000 today. The cost of maintenance, property taxes, and insurance will come to $400 per month, and they haven't even written the mortgage check yet. That will add another $1,250 at today's rate (6.5 percent, but it will probably be higher by the time you read this). True, they'll get some of that back at tax time, but still, from a monthly cash-flow basis, this represents an increase in housing costs of two and one-half times what they were shelling out back at the apartment complex. And this is to say nothing of the cost of new curtains, carpets, drapes, furniture, swing sets, and so on that inevitably get tacked on to such transactions, probably because they seem so small in comparison to the total home price itself.

No other cost tends to rise so dramatically for a new family as that of housing. The total food budget, for example, actually often declines as children come into the picture. For one thing, all those meals at Chez Provence tend to become evenings of meatloaf and mashed potatoes with peas when the baby appears. Gourmet meals cooked at home for eight of one's closest friends featuring vertical tastings of reserve California Cabernets are replaced by reheated fried chicken, eaten after the little one has finally fallen asleep.

The same principle applies to transportation. The majority of young families in America spend most of their transportation dollars on automobile-related expenses. When little Timmy comes along, it isn't unusual for this portion of the family budget to shrink as Mom and Dad tearfully give up their out-of-warranty Saab Turbo and downshift to a used Toyota minivan, saving in insurance premiums, maintenance bills, and traffic tickets on the way.

Education

There's a genuine national crisis in education. Fifty years ago, few American families even considered sending their children to private schools, especially for the elementary years. The public schools were far from perfect, but they performed an adequate job of socializing youngsters and teaching them the basics. Except for extremely wealthy families, those with distinct religious beliefs that they wished to see taught in school, and those with special-needs children, public schools were the norm.

Then came a variety of basic changes in the ethno-demographics of big-city life, a drastic loss of discipline in the classroom, and a rapidly unraveling educational process. Getting home in one piece took the place of calculus. Students weren't taught to add, but they were taught the higher metaphysics of political correctness. It became acceptable to learn everything you needed to know in kindergarten.

The net of it all was that by the early 1990s, in large cities and in many suburbs, public education had become a vast wasteland. For a plethora of reasons that may never be fully understood, the entire national public-education system—the one that had so successfully responded to Sputnik in the 1950s—could no longer provide an education, despite ever-increasing sums being lavished on the public-school monopoly.

The long-term consequences of an ill-educated population have only begun to be felt, and they'll be part of our legacy to future generations who must compete on a global stage against countries that have been willing to discipline their children to study and work hard, just as earlier generations in America did. Our overly permissive child-rearing environment, spawned by the bogus research of Margaret Mead and then broadcast by Dr. Benjamin Spock, has proven to be a disaster. Today, only 70 percent of students graduate from high school on schedule, and of these, only about half are prepared to attend a four-year college or university. According to the U.S. Department of Education, American high-school seniors now rank ninth and tenth on standardized tests in math and science against students from other developed countries. Eventually, grade inflation may be recognized as being just as corrosive to our quality of life as monetary inflation.

This is a national problem, and it's also a personal problem for the young American family. In addition to paying the property taxes that support the crumbling public schools, Mom and Dad now feel compelled to pay tuition at private or parochial schools (or have a parent homeschool, which represents a cost in the form of forgone wages). In 2000, one in ten children in the United States in grades 1 through 12 attended private schools. This costs money.

According to the National Center for Education Statistics, for the school year 1999 to 2000 (the latest year for which data is available), average tuition at religion-based schools ran $3,503 for elementary and $6,536 for secondary students. Tuition at Catholic schools ran a bit less: $2,451 and $5,845, respectively. Catholic and Jewish schools, which are often strongholds of academic excellence, tend to be a much better bargain than the North Shore Country Day School (or your neighborhood's equivalent) if you don't mind the religious component, which tends to be a pretty weak cup of tea at this point in any case. (Don't get us wrong: We *like* the religious component and wish there were a lot more of it, starting with the Ten Commandments, now better known as the Ten Lifestyle Suggestions.)

At nonsectarian schools, the tab was dramatically higher: $7,884 for elementary school and $14,638 for middle and high school. For example, the private kindergarten near your authors costs $20,000 annually, while tuition at private day high schools in Los Angeles is routinely over $25,000—to say nothing of the mandatory student fees, annual giving campaigns, and the general cost of keeping up with the rich crowd your child is captive to at schools like these. L.A. is a bargain compared to Manhattan, where the median tuition for a private high school senior is $27,200. If you want to send your little maharaja or maharani to Andover or Lawrenceville, you'll spend even more.

Now imagine that you have two, three, or four children, not just one. Multiply all of the above expenses, and you'll see immediately that you're well on your way to the poorhouse.

The jaw-dropping question is this: Where are you, young married couple, going to find the $3,000, $13,000, or $30,000 it costs every year (after taxes) to pay for 12 to 20 years of private schooling per child? Unless you work for or rob an investment bank, it's not going to be easy. Furthermore, given the risky condition of the baby boomer's retirement savings, it's going to be harder than ever to get Mom and Dad or Grandma and Grandpa to chip in for the tuition.

In today's America, you'll almost certainly have to pay in some way or another for a decent education for your children. By far the best option for young families is to buy a home (or rent) in a neighborhood that still has a functioning public-school system—one that has somehow escaped unscathed or where the parents have retaken the school from the bureaucrats and restored discipline. These schools can and do exist, although they're invariably located in the more expensive neighborhoods with higher property taxes. (Note that the reverse is not necessarily true: There are expensive neighborhoods with public schools right out of *The Asphalt Jungle*.) The house that saves its owners from having to send Junior and Sis to St. Mark's is going to cost much more than the house next to High School High, but that difference might be decisive if you have more than one child in school.

If redirected, $5,000 or $15,000 a year per child in private-school tuition goes a long way toward paying some additional property tax. It also props up the value of your home, which you stand to recoup later, rather than flying away forever, as tuition dollars do. If you have more than one child, finding a decent public school becomes financially imperative for all but the most affluent. And once you find one that you like, you'll have to get (and stay) involved, to make sure that it remains that way. If administrators see your face all the time, it will be harder for them to stick your kid with the rotten teachers.

Realtors can be counted on to rave about the local schools no matter how abysmal the test scores, so take their words with a grain of sodium chloride (or salt, as you hope they'll teach your child in science class). The Mommy mafia will have the real scoop; they can be located pushing their perambulators at the local Whole Foods. Track them down and grill them for details. Increasingly, in our No Child Left Untested world, the latest test scores (which private schools rarely deign to reveal) are available on the Internet. Do your sleuthing before you buy in the neighborhood, and above all, stop by the school for a visit. Ten minutes spent observing in the classroom will tell you all you need to know, which is often enough to ruin your day.

If you can save money and earmark it for education before the day when you have to open a vein for an anonymous bursar somewhere in private-school land, you'll be that much ahead of the game. But what if you're unable to save and simply can't afford to pay for Junior's schooling out of your current income? Is precollegiate, nonpublic school tuition a worthy cause for borrowing? The answer to that question depends on how you feel about your kids. If you believe, as most Americans do, that you have a duty to your children to send them out into the world as well prepared for the struggle as you possibly can, then a good primary education is a must, and this may well mean private school. It's sad but true.

Education should first be paid for by spending less on entertainment, housing, transportation, meals away from home, telephone bills, or anywhere that fat still lingers in the family budget. But if drastic economies in spending on Chez Louis, manicures, trips to Saint Lucia, and plasma TVs don't generate enough to pay for a school where Junior can study Shakespeare and Sis can learn calculus, then borrowing is definitely in order. But how? Obviously, you can't pay for private school with your MasterCard. Just as obviously, most banks don't have a usual category for nonpublic-school loans, and even if they did, the interest rate would be too high.

Lenders who work within banks or finance companies are very much like you and me: They want the best possible security. If at all feasible, they want to lend against both collateral and income, and they'll charge less interest if they can. That means that for most young families, the best kind of loan for a private school would be against a residence—in other words, a home equity loan will be your best bet.

Don't plan to pay for all of the children's schooling through borrowing. As your income rises over time, you should plan to control your expenditures so that, at some time in the near future, you'll be able to cover school plus the loan repayments, as well as all your other expenses, out of current income. (This doesn't mean all the loans have to be repaid completely by a time in the near future, only that you should no longer need to take out fresh ones.)

Many private and parochial schools offer at least some tuition assistance in the form of scholarship grants and loans out of their own funds, but don't count on receiving much unless your son is a star quarterback or a member of a sought-after minority group. (Your authors have friends whose adopted son is $1/16$ Cherokee. Ever since they started filling out private-school applications, they've taken to calling him "Tonto.")

The most important points to remember are these:

- You'll have to pay in some way for the education of young children.

- The family that makes advance preparation for this expense will be far ahead in terms of lightening their burden.

- Education is a legitimate and even noble reason for borrowing, but do it carefully.

- Make a plan for controlling expenses over time that allows you to cover education and loan repayments out of your current income stream.

85

It's a national disgrace that our public-school system is so weak that middle-class people not only have to pay property taxes but sometimes must sacrifice drastically to provide an education for their children. But unfortunately, this is the way things are, and we have to plan for life as it is today, not as it was yesterday.

Pay It Forward: A Few Notes on Real Estate (Again)

When a family is starting out, housing costs must bear a well-thought-out relation to present and future income. The key for the young couple is to plan in advance and to budget for the expansion of their housing well before the bassinet needs to be put into the second bedroom.

That is, the first years of work and marriage generally offer the highest discretionary income for decades to come. If you can divert as much of that money as humanly possible into saving for your house, even before you think it's necessary, you'll make the transition as painless as possible. With so many financial and emotional dislocations already attendant upon the arrival of children, it's like manna from heaven to have the biggest shift already under your belt.

What If We Can't Afford to Buy?

The alert reader may very well stroke his beard at this point and say, "This is all well and good for the couple who's managed to save enough for a down payment. It's grand for the pair who has enough earning power to pay for the additional monthly payments needed to buy their home rather than rent. But what about people like my wife and me, who are barely getting by on what we earn right now? I can't possibly afford to buy rather than rent. What about us?"

There are two answers to that line of inquiry. Answer number one is that it's simply true that there are some couples who can't buy a home in the first decade of their work lives. After all, some people earn more than others. A kindergarten teacher tends to make less than a lawyer, an artist less than a plumber. In other words, even with the equity buildup, the tax shelter, and the enforced saving that home ownership alluringly offers, many people still can't afford it.

If these individuals choose to remain in their current lines of work, they shouldn't plan to buy a house with money they don't have. After all, the point is to enhance peace of mind, not to wreck it. At some point, even if that time isn't in sight yet, rising income should eventually make it possible to move into larger digs, including possibly buying a residence. The downside of continued renting is that these folks build up no equity in their homes, plus they don't get the tax-deduction for mortgage interest, and they pass up the advantage of enforced saving.

If you can't afford to buy a home before Baby comes, you at least should make some provision to set aside enough money to rent larger quarters. This is when you should be prepared to start your family. Just as a child should be wanted in terms of the love and emotional maturity of the parents, it should also be arriving when there's enough space for it in the home and enough money to keep it in Gerber and Huggies. This means that you must keep a careful rein on every other item of expense so as to save enough for either the down payment or higher rent. It usually isn't possible to spend as much as you want on other things and also save enough to have a decent home if income is rising slowly from a low base.

Masters and Fates

There's another answer for those who fear that they won't be able to buy a house in time: Incomes aren't fixed in stone. Ever since there have been societies with marketplaces for labor, workers have been striving to upgrade their earning capacity. The secretary goes to night school to learn accountancy, while the accountant signs up for extra classes to earn a law degree. The lawyer takes advanced training in new directions for estates and trusts.

Sometimes people work two jobs. It's common for even college-educated people to moonlight in order to add to their incomes. The schoolteacher takes a post teaching PowerPoint in an adult-ed program. The nurse finds part-time work in the home of a wealthy invalid. The fledgling writer who loves clothes gets a job in a dress shop. In short, the hours that might have been spent watching *Law & Order* turn into a few extra bucks.

For the young couple preparing to start a larger family, eager to collect the savings necessary to rent or buy a larger home, the option of increasing earnings by gaining new skills or working more hours merits special attention. There's no law requiring workers to spend their evenings playing video games or watching television. In fact, many young people find greater pleasure working than watching the ten-zillionth TV situation comedy of their lifetimes.

There will be plenty of time in the future when they need the money but may not be so well prepared physically or emotionally to earn it, let alone be able to do so without paying a babysitter $10 an hour while they leave the house to earn $15 an hour. Night school leading to a better job is no crime, and a part-time job at the local Safeway isn't a prison sentence. Indeed, these acts can create the kind of financial ease that brings couples closer and makes nights more restful. Even in the inflated housing market of our time, four or five years' worth of part-time work can yield a down payment on a house or condo.

Remember that your employer can't always afford to give you all the training that you'd like. If you get your MBA (or some other useful degree) on the corporate dime, there's no guarantee that you're going to stick around long enough for the business to realize a return on its investment. Since the degree belongs to you and not to those who footed the bill, it isn't necessarily a wise use of the company's capital to pay for all of your extra education (even if sometimes they will contribute to it). However, it may well be a wise use of your *personal* capital, since the MBA travels with you wherever you go.

Of course, part-time work or school isn't for everyone. Some people work such exhausting days that they simply lack the stamina to take on a second job. Moreover, some folks love their leisure so much that they can't bear to tear themselves away for a class in accounting—that's the infinite variety of human preference. Just as there's nothing wrong with having a second income or taking classes, there's no shame in not doing so. But the young couple should be aware that working at more than one job or improving skills and productivity through education is the classic way to prepare for financial need. If you need more money for larger quarters and the arrival of Baby, part-time work can be a godsend.

More Examples

In the previous chapter, we showed how a young couple might manage their savings to acquire a house. This time, we added some babies to the picture and ran the scenarios through ESPlanner. The answer turns out to be the same as before, only more so. Median-income working couples need to spend several years saving for the down payment of their house, and then they have to live more modestly than childless couples, due to the increased expenses of their larger families. The good news is that by following this method, they can smooth out their standard of living over their lifetime. We also varied the mix, adding different numbers of babies and then making provisions for a low-cost (religion-affiliated) private school.

Once again, we used the same demographically normal couple. Some would say that this couple is so normal as to be boring, but that's okay. You don't have to invite them over for a dinner party; we're just considering their finances here. Even if you're not normal (and who among us truly is?), at least you can see how they fare and make the relevant adjustments to your situation.

Our hypothetical couple knows that they want to have a child at age 35 and buy their median house just in time to bring the infant home to the new neighborhood. How does having a baby alter their standard of living, as compared with the dual-income-no-kids (DINK) couple who bought the house in the last chapter? Remember that the DINKs were looking at a lifetime-consumption allowance (money available for everything else after housing expenses, taxes, retirement savings, and life insurance) of $43,582 constant dollars a year. For our one-child household, the average consumption allowance drops to $38,800 per year, on average.

How did our home-owning, child-bearing couple achieve this smoothed-out lifestyle? By adjusting their savings as shown in Figure 7.3. Again, the horizontal axis shows the couple's age, and the vertical axis shows how much money they need to save (positive dollar numbers) or withdraw from their savings (negative dollar numbers) in order to keep their standard of living as level as possible. Each triangle on the chart represents one year's amount of money put away or dollars withdrawn from their savings at a given age (and, for simplicity's sake, we've assumed that they're the same age).

Figure 7.3: Recommended Annual Contributions to or Withdrawals from Savings for One-Child, Median-Income Family to Maintain an Even Lifestyle when Buying a House

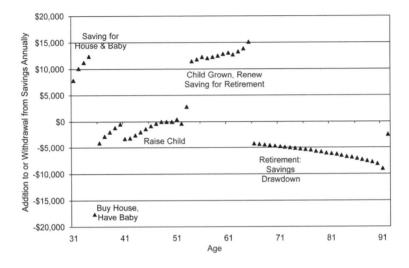

Here's their method:

- From ages 31 to 34, they save money in one of the balanced funds we mentioned in Table 4.1 (see page 44) in gradually increasing amounts, starting with about $8,000 and ending at about $12,500.

- Then at age 35, they spend most of this account for the down payment on their house. This is the outlying black triangle at the bottom of the graph. This is the same year that they have a child.

- Over the next 15 years, they dip into their balanced-fund savings a bit more in the course of bringing up Baby.

- Their savings become aggressive once the child turns 18 and decamps for his own life. (We'll discuss college in a later chapter.) This time, the money goes straight into their retirement accounts, where it can grow tax deferred.

- Finally, they retire at age 66 only to learn that Social Security has cut their benefits by 25 percent that same year. They draw down their retirement accounts steadily thereafter.

- They die, leaving their paid-off house as an inheritance for their grown child.

Don't worry about the exact dollar amounts here, just keep your focus on the big picture. This is the blueprint. With theme and variation, the same pattern holds true for every scenario that follows. Step 4 in getting your financial life is to save in advance for having children, even above and beyond the savings required to purchase a home.

More Children

What if the couple wants more children? The same template applies, but even more so. The net result is a slightly lower standard of living, because the same income is spread more thinly. While the one-child couple had a consumption allowance of $38,800 annually on average (spread among two adults and one child), the two-child couple has a consumption allowance of $36,880 a year (now covering two adults and two children).

This is quite doable, but calls for more belt-tightening initially. To smooth out their standard of living, the two-child couple needs to save more initially, starting at $10,000 and ending up at $14,500 per year in savings over a four-year period for the down payment on their median house and the initial child expenses. Then, after the kids leave, their retirement savings quickly ramp up from $12,000 to more than $15,000 dollars a year. Remember that while savings come and go under this model, their overall lifestyle is largely the same from year to year.

Want to try for child number three? This time, advance savings to the balanced fund account should first increase from $12,000 to $17,000 annually over a four-year period for the down payment on the house and (eventually) the children. Then, once the last kid has been packed off to his or her own life, your retirement savings rocket from $13,000 to $17,000 per year. Child number three decreases the family's annual consumption allowance to about $34,880 per year, now distributed among two adults and three children.

The relative dollars available for consumption every year for each of these respective families are shown in Figure 7.4.

Figure 7.4: Average Annual Dollars Available for Consumption by Median-Income Families of Differing Sizes

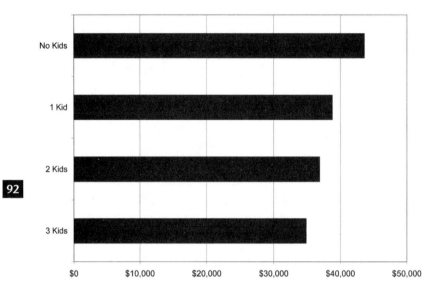

Summing Up

To recapitulate: The largest single additional out-of-pocket cost of having children is the increase in the cost of shelter, if you leave out private education at an exclusive school, which we hope that you can by the expedient buying of your residence in an area with a non-dysfunctional public school system. If, by advance planning and by judicious restraint, a young couple can save enough for a down payment somewhere that's green and put some more aside to cover the inevitable contingencies that arise when there's a little wail in the nursery, they'll be on the way to becoming a happy family.

CHAPTER 8

IN YOUR 30s

I f you're like most people (and in this respect, we hope you are), you may hope to find your income continuing to rise rapidly throughout your 30s, as shown in Figure 8.1.

Figure 8.1: Inflation-Adjusted Income in Your 30s

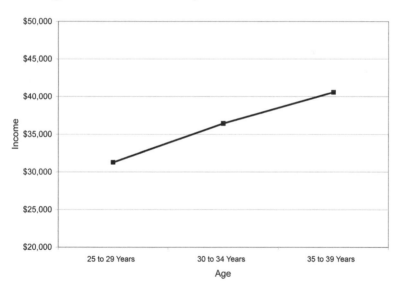

This is good news, as a rising income covers a multitude of sins and makes for a general sense of exhilaration. But while your 30s can and should be a time of happiness even beyond your 20s, there are pitfalls waiting to ensnare the unwary:

- The movement in and out of the labor force of mothers of young children

- The powerful urge to kick your lifestyle up a notch as you leave your student days behind

- The astronomical incidence of divorce

We'd better sit down and take these one by one.

Mommy's Missing Paycheck

Now, about that little problem of Mom leaving the workforce: It can be a killer. By 2004, 71 percent of mothers with children under 18 worked full- or part-time. For those with children under six at home, the figure was 62 percent.

Those working women contribute plenty to the family's take-home pay. For couples where the wife worked full-time, her contributions to the total family income were about 30 percent of the total. For older, college-educated moms, the percentage is even greater.

This means that there will be a very large downward jolt if and when the wife leaves the labor force to bring up baby. If families prepare for that shock by accumulating savings and drawing up a new spending plan so they'll be ready when Mom quits work, they'll fare better. But if they expect that by trimming a little around the edges they can adjust to a 30 percent drop in earnings at precisely a time when all other expenses are rising, they're dead wrong. This chasm can't be crossed with small changes. It must be made up by major controls on spending, the husband adding to his income in some way, large drawdowns of savings, or borrowing. It can't be done by switching to off-brand grape pop and saving used soap slivers to press into new bars.

If you already have a big enough home and sufficient savings to get you over the rough while you become a one-paycheck family, you'll smile a lot more at the baby.

The Sex-Class System and You

There's another painful note regarding mothers who leave the workforce: Once they return, they'll be shocked at how much they'll have to give up in the way of accumulated pay increases. Because they've been at home, they haven't added to their productivity or seniority. Women and men who stayed in the labor force received more money year after year as their skills and output rose. The mom who stays home teaching Junior to read won't get those raises; she'll be lucky to get the same salary she had when she left work for the obstetrics ward.

This may seem to be wildly unfair. After all, raising children is a crucial, integral part of the work of the nation. Why should women who've been doing that work be penalized for it by not getting wage increases that others did? However unfair it is, that's the way things work. It's no secret that women generally earn less than men in this country—as in all countries that have statistics. The reason for this is that women leave the labor force far more frequently and for much longer periods than men do. They don't get all the accumulated momentum of raises received by those who stay put.

While it might seem tempting to restore justice by having the government prescribe "fair" wages, remember that we don't live on an island, and our businesses must compete against countries where markets (not governments) fix wages. The net effect would be to lower the standard of living for every other American while raising lifestyles abroad. Even if you believe that our current arrangement is a gross injustice, your anger won't get the family through the financial narrows when Baby comes. The only choice is to make realistic provisions for the world as it is.

Madison Avenue's Snares and Delusions

Next, and closely allied with all of this, there's a great temptation to move up to a whole new lifestyle when the adults in a family get into their 30s. Why not? You see other 30-year-olds who have Hummers and summer cottages in the Hamptons. The young adults in advertisements, movies, and in TV shows all seem to drive fancy cars; take extreme vacations; and live in large, professionally decorated houses and penthouses. Young families in their 30s might well assume—as many do—that it's their God-given right to live just like the people they're watching every day and night. In fact, that's sort of the whole idea behind the advertisements.

This belief, however, is a trap. Human beings can only afford to live as well as they can afford to live. The appearance of another family with a certain lifestyle in a commercial is irrelevant. There's no reason at all for real, live people to imitate video or magazine people unless they can afford to and also have nothing more important to spend their money on.

If you let yourself get captured by a Madison Avenue–inspired way of life, you're shooting yourself in the foot. Because, like a rat on an exercise wheel, you'll never arrive. With more income, your aspirations will simply move up in parallel. If someone gives you a check for $50 million, within months you'll be worrying about which private jet to buy and find yourself preoccupied with redecorating mansions in three states.

What gets families into financial disaster is when they try to reach for a lifestyle that isn't affordable for people at their income level. The family sees the boats, cars, and travel, and believing that it's their right to have these goodies, they take out a home equity loan. If they try to dream their way to affluence, they wake up with real-life nightmares.

Just because that old couch is lumpy doesn't mean you can buy a new living-room suite from Knoll. Life doesn't work like that. Having neighbors who got a new Lexus doesn't mean that one fits into your budget. You can only afford one when you have enough money for it—*after* you've paid for all the major, necessary expenses, such as the education of your children and your retirement.

When income is shooting upward, there's a great temptation to spend like a drunken sailor. This isn't facing reality. You'll inevitably have large expenses to prepare for, even if they aren't staring you in the face when you shave every morning. Don't ignore the real-world limits on how much you can upgrade your lifestyle.

Instead of taking the easy way and lusting after possessions that you can't afford, why not take the road less traveled and practice the spiritual discipline of contentment. It's the only surefire get-rich-quick scheme in the world—one that brings you prosperity not just quickly but instantly. The only truly wealthy people are those who love what they have.

Divorce, American Style

Now for a few sobering thoughts about divorce: You know that 50 percent of first marriages end in divorce. We all think and hope that it won't happen to us, but it comes to people across every kind of income, educational, and even religious background. To be prepared doesn't mean having signed depositions and demands for visitation in your desk drawer. It means that if you, as a family, are about to undertake huge financial responsibilities, you might just give some thought to two questions:

1. Will this cause so much strain in a marriage that the possibility of divorce increases in an already-vulnerable age-group?

97

2. Will this be so weighty that, in the event of a divorce, life will be impossible afterward?

The first is a less threatening question, but one that even intelligent persons rarely ask themselves. Marriages can only absorb so much stress without collapsing under the weight. This includes financial anxiety.

Men and women should pause before buying a Porsche or a Poggenpohl kitchen to ask whether they can really spend that money without unduly raising the stress level within the family. If not, they should carefully weigh whether or not that purchase is so important that it outweighs the possible damage to the marriage. The real cost of any purchase isn't just the cash; it includes the stress brought on by having to pay for it. Everyone should bear that cost in mind, but men and women in the high-risk age-group for divorce should pay particular attention.

Divorce court is quite an expensive extra-cost option for a luxury car, and the most elegant Euro-style kitchen won't provide much nurturance during night after night of loneliness. In fact, the impulse to purchase such extravagances may itself indicate a desperation to find fulfillment in external possessions that should be coming from primary relationships.

Divorces rarely happen out of the blue; people who are having trouble in their marriages usually know it. For them to enter into large purchases is risky, because expensive living doesn't save a marriage. That new house or dream vacation won't do it. Instead, they'll burn through savings, and in the worst case, add another level of horror by imposing future payments upon financially strapped, newly single individuals. Purchases made by a couple or family contemplating divorce or having emotional problems should meet tests of compelling need.

Conclusions to Live By

98

The facts on being in your 30s in America are these:

- Your income will rise very fast for the first half of the decade. This should provide the wherewithal for buying a home, having and educating children, and a gradual increase to a new level of comfort in your life.

- If Mom is going to leave the workforce to raise the kids, you'll have to make substantial financial adjustments.

- Bear in mind that divorce is a major threat to Americans in their 30s, and take steps to make certain that your spending habits don't aggravate the risks.

The 30s are the period in which families can expect to move to a position of financial stability if they don't go crazy thinking that they can afford everything at once.

◢◥◣

CHAPTER 9

SAVING AND INVESTING IN YOUR 30S

H ere's where we left off with saving and investing in your 20s:

- **Cash reserves:** We recommended that you have two to six months' living expenses (depending on your job security) invested in a high-paying money market fund.

- **Retirement account:** We recommended that you keep 100 percent indexed in equities, 60 percent in the U.S. and 40 percent abroad, using low-expense index funds such as Vanguard's VTSMX for the total U.S. stock market and VGTSX for the total international stock market.

- **Other investment accounts (if any):** We recommended that you keep these in a simple, conservative, low-expense balanced mutual fund divided between stocks, bonds, and cash, warehoused at a low-cost provider such as Vanguard or Fidelity.

What needs to change now?

Cash Reserves

As everything about your lifestyle has gotten larger, you probably need to keep greater cash reserves to match, at least in absolute dollar amounts. What made up three months' living expenses when you were 25 may not quite cut it if you need to find a new job when you're 35. If you're married with kids, the prospect of a layoff is all the more consequential for everyone.

The bottom line is that you need to keep more money under the mattress to smooth over the rough patches. If you have to put a new roof on the manse, buy a new car, or whatever, you don't want to have to sell stock at an inopportune time. So boost the cash reserves so that you have enough to cover these types of emergencies. The same rules apply as before: as little as two months' living expenses if you have a secure job with a large corporation and as much as six months' expenses if you're self-employed, your work situation is more tenuous, or if it might be difficult for you to find new employment for whatever reason. What has likely changed since you last visited this category is your expenses: They've gotten bigger as you've grown older, so you need to increase your cash reserves to match your potential short-term liabilities.

Retirement Accounts

Because you're a bit older, with fewer years until retirement, you have less time to recover from a whopping loss in the stock market. You need to dampen the market's vicissitudes, even if it means losing a little bit of investment performance on the upside to do so. This is a worthwhile trade-off. We recommend adding a 20 percent bond position, for an 80 percent equity/20 percent fixed income approach, as shown in Figure 9.1.

Figure 9.1: 30s Asset Allocation

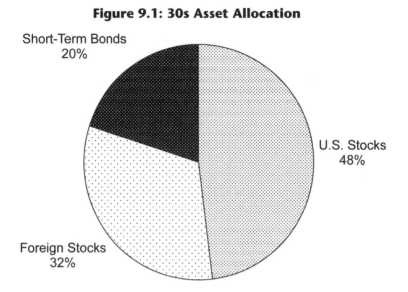

What kind of bonds should you add? If your 401(k) has the usual terrible menu of stock fund offerings, you won't believe how bad the fixed income offerings will be. The best choice would be a low-expense short-term bond index fund, or a fund that tracks the Lehman Brothers Aggregate Bond Index. Sometimes these latter funds are labeled "Total U.S. Bond Market" or something similar. Barring that, an "Inflation-Protected Bond Fund" would be a good pick. But stay away from junk bonds (aka "High Yield" bonds), "Stable Value Funds," and "Long-Term Bond Funds." You may have to punch the fund tickers into **Morningstar.com** to learn more about them. You're looking for a bond fund with as low an expense ratio as possible, with short maturities (or low duration) and high credit quality.

How much should you be saving toward retirement as a percentage of your current salary? Our best answers are shown in Table 9.1. If we learn of better ones, we'll post them to the Stein-DeMuth Website.

Table 9.1: Recommended Savings Rates as % of Current Gross Salary		
If You Have in Savings:	You Should Save:	
	Age 30	Age 35
No Retirement Savings	10%	14%
Savings = ¼ of Salary	8%	12%
Savings = ½ of Salary	6%	10%
Savings = 1 Year's Salary	3%	7%
Savings = 2 Years' Salary	0%	0%

And as a reality check, the amount of retirement-earmarked savings that you should have at these ages is shown in Table 9.2.

Table 9.2: Are Your Retirement Savings on Track?	
Multiple of Current Salary You Should Have in Savings	
Age	Retirement Savings
30	0.3 – 0.5
35	1

Investment Accounts

If you haven't already married, bought a house, and had children, there is a high probability that at some point during your 30s you will. You might be able to fob off the wedding expenses on your (or your bride's) parents, although they might have been happier to pony up for the big affair if you'd married when you were age 21. If you're really lucky, maybe they'll even contribute toward the down payment for your house. Probably, though, you'll have to reach deep into your own pockets for these expenditures. This means that you'll need plenty of money in your taxable investment accounts.

These expenses are so probable that we're willing to let you off the hook from your retirement savings (although you should at least contribute enough to capture any employer match in your 401(k), if humanly possible), *with the proviso that you put the same money instead into your taxable investment account.* We still like the generic, low-expense, conservative balanced funds we recommended back in Table 4.1 (on page 44). Figure 9.2 shows how much a dollar invested in one of these funds every year might be worth over time. Under ordinary circumstances, after five years of regular contributions, you get the sixth year more or less for free.

**Figure 9.2: Saving $1 per Year in a
Balanced Fund Gives You . . .**

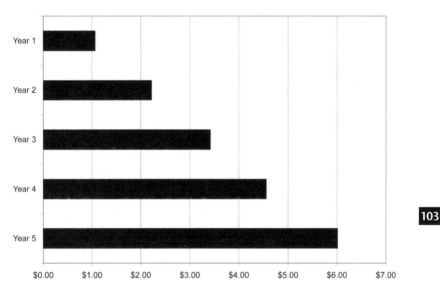

103

Your goal is to have as much money as possible in this account for the down payment on your house. The ideal is 20 percent of your home's price, but in today's inflated housing market that may not be possible. Our examples have had to assume a 10 percent down payment, just to make the whole deal doable for middle-class folks with no fairy godmother. Add a child (which you'll also want to plan for), and you want to have around half of your combined pretax salaries in savings. For two kids, you would want two-thirds of your combined paychecks in your taxable investment accounts, and if you contemplate three children, three-quarters of your salaries. The only way for most people to get to this point is by saving a big chunk (in the 10 to 20 percent range) of pretax income for four or five years in a row, and then letting the market return on investment contribute the rest.

These figures are ballpark estimates for people with median

incomes. If you earn more, while it's possible that you may need to set aside less, it's equally possible that you won't, because you're likely to want a more-than-medium-expensive house. You'll also end up spending more than average in raising your child.

These are the big, grown-up expenses that young Americans face today. The best way to pay for them is by saving in advance. If you blindly wander into buying a house and having a baby, you'll find it extremely difficult to make ends meet without getting into trouble with credit cards and every other kind of debt.

As a trade-off, the middle-class American lifestyle is the envy of the world. To quote from the outstanding book *Can America Survive?* (also by your authors):

> The average middle-class person in the United States today lives like a king . . . actually, better than any king of yore—better than Caesar, better than Napoleon, and better than the Rockefellers or Carnegies or Vanderbilts in the 1890s. Andrew Carnegie couldn't go to Paris for the weekend; he couldn't even call London to check on the stock market. He couldn't hear the Berlin Philharmonic unless he traveled to Berlin. He couldn't order a gin and tonic with ice cubes in it, or eat watermelon on Christmas Day. He couldn't take an aspirin if he had a headache. He couldn't get Thai or Mexican or Italian or Indian takeout, and there weren't 50 flavors of coffee to drink on every street corner.
>
> If he had a cavity (very likely, since both his drinking water and toothpaste were unfluoridated), the trip to the dentist would be unforgettable. No medicines could help him with obesity, hair loss, or erectile dysfunction; and God help him if he really became ill. There was no open-heart surgery, no anticancer surgery or medications, no antibiotics or antivirals; if his child developed black diphtheria, nothing could be done. Half the population back in Carnegie's day died of contagious diseases, resulting in an average life expectancy of 49 years for males. (p. 20)

If your family can measure your reach by your grasp, at least financially, you'll avoid a great number of problems, and wonderfully, the stage will be set for a decade you can look back upon happily for the rest of your life.

CHAPTER 10

A Word on Insurance

There's yet another thing you need in your life once you have a family and a home, a line item that we've glossed over until now. You need life insurance.

If you're a single man or woman, or even a young couple without children, you don't urgently need life insurance—in fact, you may not need it at all. But once you've obliged yourself to put a roof over the heads of your children, you must provide some protection for them in case you or your spouse goes to heaven sooner than expected. If you pass from this earthly vale, there will be a giant economic hole in the family's picture. Not only will there be a catch in her throat when Sis says grace at Thanksgiving dinner, but there will be a giant catch when your family opens the bills each month and stares at the blank space on the bank statement where your paycheck used to be automatically deposited.

That's why America has a $3 trillion insurance industry: to make certain that deceased moms and dads can help their spouses and kids maintain a decent standard of living. The question about insurance is seldom about whether to have it; the question is what kind.

There are four basic types of life insurance:

- **Whole life** is the favorite of agents. It provides a prescribed death benefit and has a residual and growing cash value as premiums are paid over time.

- **Term life** has a prescribed death benefit but no cash value at any time if there's no death. It might be thought of as a simple bet about whether or not the insured will die within the term of the policy.

- **Universal life** is a combination of term and whole life. It provides a cash value and a prescribed benefit, but the cash value is much lower than in whole life, while the payoff upon death is much higher than the same premiums would buy with whole life. The universal life policy takes some of your premiums and invests them in a term policy, then takes the rest of your premiums and invests them in a whole life policy. That is, some of your premiums build up a cash value at a rate of interest prescribed by the insurance company.

- **Variable life** is really a variant of universal life. It takes some of your premiums and puts them in a term policy, then takes the rest of your premiums and puts them into stock or bond mutual funds. The policy pays out a prescribed amount upon death. It acquires a cash value determined by the performance of the stocks or bonds in the whole life component of the policy. In a rising market, such policies are popular and can pay off well. In a long-term bear market, they'll be disappointing.

Which one should a young family in their 30s have? There's fairly general consensus, even among insurance agents, that if a family can save on their own, then whole life isn't for them. The rate of return given by insurance companies on premiums paid under whole life tends to be inferior to investing the same principal on your own.

If whole life is no great deal, then that fact casts a shadow across universal life as well. After all, why buy even a partial whole life policy if whole life isn't a bargain?

What about variable life? Unfortunately, a big caution light glows over any life insurance plan that ostensibly provides for

106

goals other than insuring your life. After all, your goal in buying this product is to provide money after your death. To the extent that insurance companies try to piggyback their goals upon yours, their efforts may hijack yours.

If you focus on your need—to insure your life—and concentrate on how to do that most economically, you'll almost certainly choose term life. Per dollar of benefit, it's by far the cheapest of any method of insurance. Intelligent persons have spent their entire lives trying to figure out the most efficient way to buy insurance, and their advice has been so consistent that it has become a cliché: "Buy term and put the savings above whole life in your own investments." This is notwithstanding the fact that every insurance agent you talk to will have the opposite advice. They want to sell whole, universal, and variable life policies because these offer much larger commissions. But people who study these things without any commissions to earn say, "Buy term and invest the rest."

Coming to Terms

107

There are now two types of term policies:

1. **Annual renewable term:** This policy (which you might buy directly online from TIAA-CREF without going through a broker, for example) starts off cheap but gets more expensive year by year as you age, and your risk of dying thereby increases. For reasons that will be explained in a moment, we have a slight preference for this type of policy.

2. **Level premium term:** This policy (which you might buy online without a front-end load from Ameritas Direct, for example; see our Website for a link) amortizes the expected price over some predetermined period, such as 10, 15, or 20 years.

You might also be fortunate enough to have life insurance offered as a subsidized benefit through your place of employment, in which case the rates may be even more advantageous.

Since the most cost-effective route is to buy the insurance policy yourself, rather than having some broker like Robert Young in *Father Knows Best* hold your hand through the process, you also need to check out the creditworthiness of the insurance carrier you use, especially if you're dealing with a company that isn't a household name. You can visit the Websites of independent raters of insurance companies, such as A.M. Best, Duff & Phelps, Moody's Investors Service, Standard & Poor's, and Weiss Research. Each has its own rating system, so grades aren't comparable from one rater to the next.

How Much Should You Get?

Of course, you have to determine not only what kind, but how much, life insurance you need. This is no small matter. Researchers report that a tour of 48 Web-based calculators offered an almost uselessly wide range of answers. There are also rules of thumb, estimates that suggest that you should have an insurance benefit anywhere from 6 to 10 (one expert recommends 20) times your current earnings. Apparently, this isn't an exact science.

To make matters worse, the risks of being underinsured are considerable. Studies have shown that roughly one-fifth of secondary earners (translation: wives) would be thrust into poverty by the deaths of their underinsured husbands, and another one-fifth would have to substantially reduce their quality of life in order to get by. Husbands: Imagine that your boss called you into the office and told you that he was going to cut your salary by 20 percent. You'd be stunned; you might even grow to resent him. Don't put your bereaved wife in this predicament.

To further complicate matters, your need for insurance doesn't remain static. Instead, it diminishes over time. Children grow up and leave home, Social Security kicks in, and the mortgage gets paid off. As these events occur, you don't need to provide as much replacement income in order for your survivors to maintain their same standard of living.

Figures 10.1 to 10.3 show the life insurance needs for our median-income working couples with one, two, and three children, from the gospel according to ESPlanner. Remember that he's 31 and earns $38,000, while she's the same age and earns $31,000. The first baby comes along in five years, and the others follow two years apart.

Figure 10.1: Life Insurance Needs for a Median-Income Family of Three

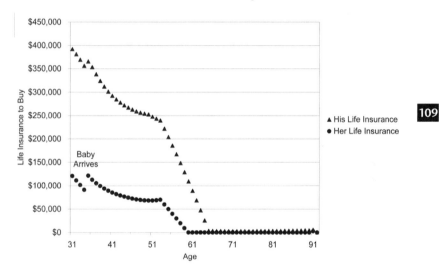

**Figure 10.2: Life Insurance Needs for
a Median-Income Family of Four**

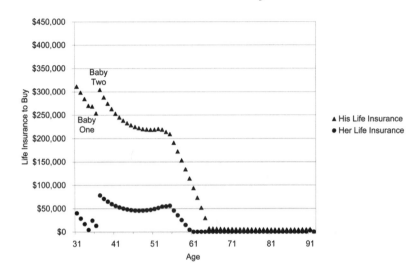

**Figure 10.3: Life Insurance Needs for
a Median-Income Family of Five**

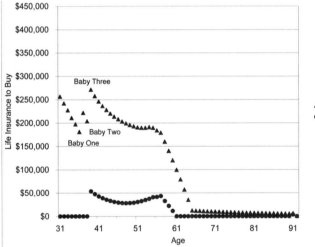

Impossible . . . but True!

A striking finding is that the more children a family has, the less life insurance it actually needs. The bittersweet reason is that the higher these fixed expenses, the lower the average standard of living the family enjoys at the same income level, so less insurance is required to maintain it over the survivor's remaining lifetime.

Keep in mind that these findings are only suggestive and that your insurance needs will undoubtedly vary from these examples. Short of purchasing the ESPlanner software yourself and plugging in your unique situation (which in itself might be a great present for yourself and your family in terms of peace of mind), it will be difficult to make the insurance calculation with precision. You might want to try a few Web-based applets and then punt. If you have to, err on the side of overinsuring. For most people, life insurance is comparatively inexpensive, and it will provide your loved ones with a heaven-sent return in the event that it's needed.

111

Other Insurance

While life insurance is a vital part of your financial picture, it's not the only insurance product you'll need.

— Naturally, you'll require **car insurance** (especially if you drive a car). You can get multiple quotes in minutes from **www.quicken.com/insurance** and **www.insweb.com**.

— You'll also need **health insurance.** The best way to get this is through your work, because it's subsidized by your employer, the company's ability to negotiate group rates, and the tax code (for the present, anyway). It becomes far more expensive to purchase this product for yourself as an individual policyholder. If you don't have insurance, you'll pay five to ten times as much for health care as people who have it through their place of employment, for the simple reason that there's no HMO or insurance company negotiating favorable rates on your behalf.

Health insurance will be relatively inexpensive to get when you're young and healthy, but the costs soar as you get older. If you wait until you're sick to buy it, you'll find that it has become prohibitively expensive and covers very little—if any policy is available to you at all.

—You'll also want to have **disability insurance.** This is frequently a perk at work but becomes more important if you're self-employed. This product isn't cheap because there's a moral hazard (owners of such policies might be tempted to claim disability to collect whether they're really disabled or not), and claims are expensive when they do occur. If you have a family depending on you, there may be no way around having to pay for such a policy.

— Whether you rent or buy your home, you'll need either **renter's** or **home-owner's insurance.** Be sure to specify that you want replacement-value coverage for your possessions. This is far more expensive, but it's the only kind to get—unless you want to replace your wardrobe that was lost in the fire by buying a new one at the Salvation Army thrift store.

In all matters, set deductibles high to save money, and file claims as infrequently as possible. Insurance is best used to cover calamities. It becomes very expensive if you try to use it for everyday peccadilloes. If you abuse your insurance company, they'll drop you like a hot potato, and then just try getting someone else to write a policy for you. Cover the nickel-and-dime items yourself, and save insurance for the day when you might really need it.

◢◣◢

CHAPTER 11

CAREER ADVICE

The basic relationship between income and consumption over a lifetime often leads to suffering and frustration because the balance is out of control for so many people. We want to help you establish a more harmonious relationship between earnings and expenditure by predicting what your likely income curve will be, and then relating it to your probable expenses so that you can line up the planets.

So far, most of our suggestions have been about controlling your consumption so that it doesn't race ahead of your income. The goal has been to establish a program of savings to provide for your retirement, a cushion for emergencies, and a head start toward buying a home and providing for children in order to give you a sense of safety in your financial life. We want to keep you from getting so hopelessly in the soup that you have to spend the rest of your young-adult life bailing yourself out.

In the service of that effort, one major fact of life—and response to it—has been barely mentioned. Back when we were describing Jane Q. Colgrad and her employer, the Pygmy Athletic Shoe Company, we talked about why the incomes of young Americans tend to rise so dramatically. It had to do with learning one's job more thoroughly, gaining expertise to do tasks better, and generally becoming more productive so that you add more value for your employer. In turn, this led to the corporation's need to pay you more in order to keep you from taking your expertise and increased productivity elsewhere. So far, so good.

In fact, the income of most young adults is destined to rise substantially. But the fact that the average goes up doesn't necessarily mean that *your* income will increase comparably. It's sad but true that just as some incomes will grow far more rapidly than the average, some will increase far less. This isn't a good situation for those persons falling below the trend line. No one wants to earn less than his or her peers, and certainly no one wants to be short of money. The question is, what on earth can you do if your income isn't keeping pace? How can you bootstrap yourself back up?

The first thing is to understand that *the reason your income isn't rising as rapidly as you'd like is because there isn't sufficient competition for your labor.* This seems cold, and it may even sound insulting, but it's actually neither. Almost no one's wages rise beyond inflation unless people in authority believe that the employee may be hired away by someone else. This is such a fact of life that it even holds true in the government, where a worker will get a small raise if he simply punches the clock. The big increases come from a boss's fear that the employee will get lured away. Even if that's a highly contingent and far-removed threat, operating mostly on a theoretical level, it still has a powerful application in every job, because it's very costly and difficult to hire and train new workers.

There can be two basic reasons why there's inadequate danger of being hired away from your job.

1. There's a problem with your personal work.
2. There's a lack of competition in the field.

Since no one who would take the trouble to buy and read a book like this would be likely to perform poorly on their job, we'll focus on the general lack of competition for labor in your field.

Why Aren't They Fighting Over You?

Here's a truism you can stitch into a sampler (paraphrased from Warren Buffett): It's better to be mediocre in a great business than to be great in a mediocre business. A great business might be defined here as one that pays people well. Teaching kindergarten is undoubt-edly rewarding on a personal level, but it isn't a great business. Robbing banks can temporarily pay a lot of money, but over a life-time it actually has a low rate of pay, so it, too, is a bad bet. Being a priest or a rabbi is great work but usually pays a lousy salary.

On the other hand, jobs where you work close to a big stream of money and are employed in directing that flow toward your company tend to pay well. These are likely to be very good busi-nesses. This might mean working as a development officer for a philanthropic foundation or as a sales manager for a financial-ser-vices company. Even if you're terrible at running a motion-picture company, you still might be hired at a stupendous salary because almost no one knows how to run such an operation at all.

When we say that there's a lack or competition for individuals in your field, that can imply different scenarios. For example, there might a be government-mandated lack of competition for people in your field. If you're a census taker and Congress has just cut funding for the Census Bureau, this may result in a hiring freeze. You can't be lured out of your department and placed somewhere else within the bureau because no other department will have any money for a new employee. The whole dismal stream of events means that your bosses know that they can keep you in your current job at the same pay. That is an example of the clearest possible kind of government-enforced ban on competition for your labor.

A slightly more familiar situation is that of teachers in states undergoing budget shortfalls. As a matter of state policy, there may be restrictions on how much instructors can be paid and then limitations on how big a raise they can get. Moreover, in this field, there's little financial competition from private schools, which generally pay even less than public schools. Again, this is the result of a sanctioned monopoly on competition in your field. Government action has made it impossible for any other part of the school system to hire you away from where you work now, artificially keeping a lid on your pay for reasons having nothing to do with your abilities.

Another reason could be the state of employment in declin-ing industries. If you work as a designer of ashtrays, for example, there's likely to be only small demand for any additional workers in your field. Smoking is a habit that (mercifully) is becoming rare. There are already many ashtrays in existence—too many, in fact. The vogue for those that are artistically designed has disappeared. You may do excellent work, but there will be little demand for the services of even a really top-drawer ashtray designer. The airlines and American car manufacturers are two currently troubled industries that come to mind in this regard. And if the housing boom busts, there will be a lot of newly minted Realtors reading the help-wanted ads as well.

Here's another scenario: You may work in a declining part of America. If you're a receptionist in Dallas three months after the price of oil has dropped by $25 per barrel, your pay is likely to remain fixed for some time to come. After all, everyone in Dallas will have fallen on hard times, and the need for receptionists is likely to be considerably lower than the demand for bankruptcy referees.

In any of these cases, you may be kept at your job at the same—or even lower—pay. Your present employer will know that it doesn't need to keep giving you raises, whatever your increased productivity, because you're just not going to be hired away.

116

Deciding on a Course of Action

These forces that restrain your pay are impersonal, but the effects on you will be extremely personal. For this reason, it's important not to confuse the two issues. If your income isn't keeping pace with the averages, this isn't the result of a conspiracy—nor is it your fault.

If you're one of those persons who looks at others succeeding around you and wonders where you went wrong, you have a number of choices. One option might be to reconcile yourself to your fate and look for other sources of satisfaction in your life. Another idea is to find a ladder to your desired curve of rising income. Or you might decide to employ a combination of reconciliation and action.

The first thing to realize is this: When you think of how to concoct a lifetime financial strategy for harmonizing your earnings with your consumption, neither side of the equation is written in permanent ink. We've already examined a number of strategies to alter your life so that you don't make the typical mistakes in spending committed by the average man or woman. By the same token, there are a number of routes to dragging yourself up from the dreary statistics about teachers' pay, declining industries, stagnant geographic regions, and below-expected earnings, and all of them can affect your income.

If You Adore Your Work

The first step is to consider whether you're working at the kind of job you love regardless of its pay. Are you so enamored of your career that you prefer to stay in it, more or less independent of the salary? Do you wake up in the middle of the night thanking your lucky stars that you get to spend your days throwing pots, guiding tours at an art museum, or teaching stroke victims to walk? Does your work feel like the best time you could possibly have with your clothes on?

If you answer yes to these questions, you're probably going to have to reconcile yourself to not getting raises as fast as those who have jobs that they may not love as much. The plain fact is that some of the most wonderful, interesting, exciting, and worthwhile occupations don't pay well. If that's your position, you must prepare yourself to live under more restricted circumstances than others do. In essence, you're being rewarded with personal satisfaction more than with money. You'll just have to remember that you can't spend what you aren't paid. Your knowledge of art and music derived from that low-income job teaching piano can be spent in conversation or letters or thought. It can't be redeemed for a designer suit or a trip to the Seychelles. We all have hard choices to make. If you choose to enter and stay in a low-paying field, it has consequences.

If you know for certain that your income will lag, you must live with frugality. It's great to enjoy your work, and it's noble to exist on a meager salary for love of your career, but you have to live far more carefully than people who aren't making these sacrifices—that's the

117

meaning of sacrifice. We've heard college professors lament that the people with money (that is, nonacademics) have no taste, while the people with good taste (that is, themselves) have no money. You may be able to write a coffee-table book about the furniture of Charles Rennie Mackintosh, but you won't be able to afford a Charles Rennie Mackintosh coffee table.

For most young Americans, however, the intrinsic rewards from their work are not so great that they outweigh every other consideration, such as . . . pay.

If You're Willing to Make a Change

Most young adults are ready to change jobs at the drop of a chapeau in order to improve their incomes. And in fact, they do so with great regularity. The key points to remember are these:

118

1. Don't rely on the law of averages to lift your income. If you want to get up to the average income level, you may have to go out and hustle up some decently paid work. It won't inevitably happen by itself, as much as you'd like it to.

2. The same dynamics that make for low-paying jobs— absence of competition for your labor—suggest where lucrative positions are to be found. They're in markets and industries where there's high competition for labor.

3. When things aren't going well financially, the temptation is inevitably to personalize your distress and feel sorry for yourself. This is a great mistake. Self-pity here (as everywhere) is a black hole that only leads to more of the same. The key is to understand the larger economic forces shaping your situation and then swim with the current rather than fighting it. There's absolutely no shame in getting out of a situation that isn't working for you. It doesn't mean that you're a failure or a loser; not every oil well that's drilled produces a gusher. The smart move is to cut your losses and move on. That's the American way.

You can and should do all you can to get an income that will rise at least as fast as the average. Our labor market is highly fluid, and people can and do change jobs for the better every day. Foreign citizens are willing to endure brutal conditions to get to the United States and gain access to our employment markets. It would be foolish for you, who are already here, not to take advantage of the same national resources.

The Exit Interview

If you do decide to move on, remember that "exit interviews" are only for the benefit of your employer and not for you. These should never be used as an occasion to vent your frustrations or backstab anyone. Be sure to only have polite, noncommittal, and above all, brief things to say about your experience and why you're moving on.

If you're leaving a ghastly work situation, your employer should exit this interview without a clue. Express your gratitude for being given a chance to be part of the team, and talk vaguely of your desire to explore new horizons, climb every mountain, and ford every stream or the need to spend more time with your family.

Under the cosmic and immutable law of karma, anyone you criticize will one day be in an important position of power over your life. He'll be called for a reference. He'll run into someone at a golf outing who's thinking of giving you a promotion. It will turn out that his spouse is the admissions director at the school that you want your child to attend. There are no exceptions to this rule. Never burn bridges. Also, when you leave, don't take so much as a paper clip that isn't yours. Bad behavior here is extremely tacky and will be remembered forever. If you can show some class while under duress, the rest will be easy.

119

Taking the Plunge

Keep in mind that the possibilities are vast. If you're a school teacher in a district teetering on the edge of bankruptcy, you can and should realize that you're free to leave the school, move away from the area, change your occupation, and generally do any number of things to make your life easier in the long run. The junior-high mathematics teacher can become an IT manager; the unemployed mechanic in Hamtramck can become the owner of an Audi repair shop in Beverly Hills. By moving to areas where there's high competition, you can and will shift your income function upward.

It won't be easy. There's a natural reluctance to step off the career treadmill upon which you find yourself at any given moment. For a teacher, the obstacles involved in becoming an engineer look immense; to the engineer, the challenges in becoming a manager look daunting. But there's almost nothing more expected and more frequently done in this country than changing industries, locations, and employers. This is a society in which workers, especially young ones, are expected to switch careers to make more money.

In fact, the whole capitalist system is based upon flows of labor into and out of positions that pay more or less as others want more or less of what the jobs produce. Do we want more home computers? San Jose booms. Do we consume less natural gas? Young people leave Bartlesville. Are adults reading less? Editors become professors. Are fewer children going to college? Professors become accountants. Are manufacturing jobs outsourced to China? Machine operators become contractors. This kind of change is, of course, far more difficult and painful on a personal level than on a national scale (where it works surprisingly well).

The point is this: Situating yourself to earn more is something society not only tolerates, but encourages. Where you stand relative to the income of your age-group is determined not only by huge aggregate movements, but also by your own energy, flexibility, and imagination. Luck plays its part as well, but you can help make your own luck. We'd all prefer a life where everything falls neatly into place, yet our forebears who pulled up roots and emigrated to

America (however recently or long ago) took an enormous leap of faith with their lives. We should summon the same spirit within ourselves when circumstances dictate.

When you find work that fully engages you, the rewards are personal as well as financial. As the saying goes, find something that you love doing, and you'll never work another day in your life.

◢◣◢

CHAPTER 12

SINGLE 30s

Have you noticed how people are delaying marriage these days? The average man waits until he's 27 to get married for the first time; the average woman, until she's 25. After their mid-30s, their chances of getting married start to trail off significantly. By the age of 25, 32 percent of men have been married, and 77 percent have done so by the age of 35. But 20 years later, only another 13 percent have tied the knot. It's the same story for women: 50 percent have married by the age of 25, 84 percent by 35 . . . but only an additional 6 percent will get married by the time they reach 55. Ten percent of society will never marry, period—and this isn't just the gay population.

Here are a few more statistics to wrap your brain around:

- Percentage of first marriages that end in divorce: 50 percent

- Median age at first divorce (males): 30.5 years

- Median age at first divorce (females): 29 years

- A disconcerting note about children: Fully 23 percent of all children under the age of 18 live with their mothers only. Single moms comprise 9.2 percent of all U.S. households.

And one final statistic: The average woman's living standard drops 45 percent following divorce. This means that her earning, spending, and savings decisions will be, for the most part, limited, painful, and unglamourous. Thomas Hobbes described life in a state of nature as solitary, poor, nasty, brutish, and short. For single mothers, he was painfully close to the mark.

If Possible, Stay Competitive

What about the likely curve of income for single 30-year-olds? For men, the curve of rising income is likely to be steep. Single women without children can expect about the same dramatic rise in income. The growth of productivity, expertise, and contacts will make 30- to 34-year-old men and women very good hiring bets. That will lead to an attendant demand either to lure them away or to keep them happy where they are by making them offers that they can't refuse. Either course will keep their income and raises up.

124

The woman with children, however, can expect such high pay only if she stays in the labor force. When women leave the payroll to have children and care for them, their seniority vanishes, and their rapidly rising pay goes with it. Women or men who frequently leave the labor force and then return to it without getting any new training will find themselves left behind by the 30s' pay-escalation gravy train.

These people can wind up late in life with far lower earnings than they had earlier. The worker who loses his or her seniority; fails to accrue knowledge or improved skills and contacts; and in addition can no longer command a premium for youth, energy, and an implicit option on a long and loyal attachment to his or her employer can wind up with the worst of all worlds. This person will have low pay and little time or opportunity for improvement.

This is an argument for spending any time you're out of the labor force improving your skills and learning, two acts that can definitely be done by men and women in almost all circumstances. Employers will often pay more of a premium—that is, make your income curve rise faster—for employees with education versus those with experience, even if the schooling isn't traditional. If you lack a college diploma, when you return after an absence from work with a certificate of mastery in Microsoft Word, Excel, and PowerPoint, you'll find that you've become an indispensable asset to your employer.

Single Women

Should a single woman have a certain amount of savings when she's in her 30s? Everyone should have savings. Life is filled with challenges and opportunities. If the boss comes in, puts his hand on your knee, and says that he wants to talk about a raise, you need to be able to walk out the door (and go straight to your sexual-harassment lawyer). The single woman with savings has what are impolitely called "F— you" options that the woman living from paycheck to paycheck simply doesn't.

The desirable amount of savings varies, depending upon how certain and settled your job is. The general rule for families is to have six months' worth of expenses set aside. Since a single woman without dependents can obviously cut back far more than a family of four, she shouldn't need that much. But the equivalent of three months' current income in a money market account is a minimum that will give you peace of mind and the opportunity to make career jumps without passing out from hunger. If you haven't been able to accumulate that much, something is definitely wrong on either the savings or spending side.

The single woman with children should have an even simpler rule about savings: She should save as much as possible. The funds will come in very, very handy. Having small children is like having little machines for generating unforeseen and expensive bills. She'll need something to cushion the blows.

Again, there's no maximum amount, within reason, for the single mother to put away. If she can save several months' worth of income, she'll be happy at some future date when the doctor tells her that her son needs an ear operation and her insurance has a $1,000 deductible. Savings, for this individual, are the solvent

125

that makes a smooth passage through life possible. A lack in this area, while totally understandable, is like having crushed glass underfoot.

Single Men

Luckily for single men in their 30s, there's almost no other group in society that's so readily employed. In the minds of employers, these guys are finished with the recklessness of their 20s but still have youth and energy, and they're full of the kind of knowledge that will lead to major productivity gains in the future.

That means a man in his 30s will have an easier time finding a job than almost any other age and sex combination. This obviously has implications for how long a man in his 30s should expect to be between jobs if he's laid off, and therefore for how much extra money he needs to have in the bank.

While everyone should have enough to cover the unexpected, some people need ready cash more than others. If a family of four should have six months' income saved and a single woman should shoot for three months' pay, a single man could probably get by with two months' income stashed away. Ironically, this is exactly the same person who can probably save one year's income without too much difficulty. To him that hath shall be given, says the Bible, and that certainly applies to single men in their 30s as far as money is concerned. Such men are able to have large savings, do not need large savings, and generally remind us of the banks that will only lend to customers who don't need a loan.

To Sum Up

Single thirtysomethings sans children can count on rapidly rising incomes unless they leave the workforce sporadically and fail to improve their education or training. They can enjoy the ecstasy of rising income and the opportunity to feel safe and secure about money. They need not expect any sudden financial shocks such as divorce or private schools for the kids. If they can pull together the money, they should try to buy a home. But if they can't readily swing this, then they shouldn't throw everything else away trying to purchase something they can't afford and don't need.

Single mothers in their 30s shouldn't expect to get their heads far above water. They shouldn't tackle house payments that will put a strain on their finances—and will eliminate their ability to deal with any unforeseen events from a position of strength. There are few things worse than not having money when you need it—that much is Financial Life 101.

◢◥◣

CHAPTER 13

LATE 30s

The Age of Limits

Trees don't grow to the sky, and salaries don't keep rising at ever-faster rates for young and middle-aged Americans. As a general proposition, the rate of income growth begins to slow down drastically after the age of 35. Figure 13.1 tells the story.

Figure 13.1: Inflation-Adjusted Income in Your Late 30s

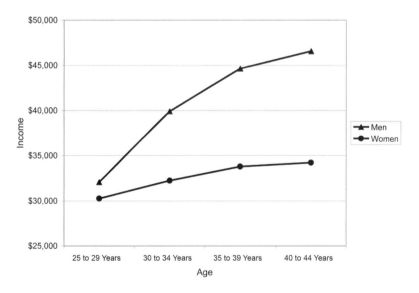

What happened? Income grew at super-rapid rates up to age 34 largely because of:

- Growing expertise on the job

- Rising productivity due to increasing knowledge and skills

- A premium for youth, health, and energy

- An implicit bonus for presumed loyalty and growth of ability

But when Americans start to hit their mid-30s, several things occur:

- The most important parts of their jobs have probably already been learned. The additional bits of knowledge available reach a point of diminishing returns, possibly costing more to acquire than they're worth in terms of productivity.

- New employees can be hired straight from school with the knowledge that employers need built-in at no extra cost, so to speak.

- A portion of what the 35-year-old employee knows may have been rendered obsolete by time and circumstance and the appearance of new techniques, players, and rules within the field.

- The implicit bonus for performance and longevity within the firm diminishes as employees prove not to be quite as much of an asset as their employers once thought they'd be.

- Most heartrending, some of what was once an implicit premium for being young is now gone, as youth itself is going. . . .

All these events conspire to reduce the rate of pay raises even for married men and single women who have never left the labor force. The increases that do occur aren't the stupendous gains that were made back in the salad days.

The Changing Center of Gravity

To see how and why all this happens, look at our old friend Jane Q. Colgrad at the Pygmy Athletic Shoe Company. She's been doing just great, finding the cheapest suppliers and best distributors and figuring out how to invest any spare cash that's lying around at the office. She's learned how to get along well with the out-of-town buyers for Macy's and Bloomingdale's. In other words, she's doing well for herself and her employers.

Over in Manila, however, a startling development has taken place. A small Filipino manufacturer of athletic shoes has built a factory with Swiss financing. That facility uses robots to make shoes out of woven palm fronds; there isn't one single human being on the floor. The manufacturer can undercut any American, Japanese, Chinese, or Korean manufacturer—and do so with a high-quality product.

Not only that, but at the same time, the U.S. Congress has passed new legislation about the importation of shoes made from palm fronds. The regulations are extremely complex, and it takes a lawyer to understand them. In addition, it happens that the new buyer from the May Department Stores Company is a young kid from Harvard who likes to do business only with other young kids from Harvard whenever possible.

All of a sudden, the center of gravity of the athletic shoe business has shifted. Jane Q. Colgrad still knows lots of important facts, but much of her knowledge is becoming out-of-date. She could learn about the new stuff, but she's set in her ways by now, and she feels (with some justice) that she shouldn't have to run as hard as a young kid simply to keep in place. There's a new MBA in the office, so Jane delegates to him the important task of finding out about how to make shoes with robot labor. The kid's a hustler. He learns everything there is to know and is soon out making deals to build robot plants in New Guinea. Meanwhile, Jane's still tending to the old-fashioned human-worker plants in Bethpage, New York, and Osaka, Japan.

The new MBA has a friend who's a lawyer at Hale and Dorr. This guy happens to know a great deal about the latest legislation bearing on importation of palm-woven athletic shoes. As it turns out, he also boarded at Choate with the new buyer from the May Department Stores Company. Pretty soon, the new MBA has an impregnable web of connections dealing with the latest developments in the athletic-shoe business. He's taking that old ball and running with it, while Jane Q. Colgrad whines about how much more successful the new guy is than he deserves to be.

When the raises are passed out, Jane's is no longer anywhere near as good as the new guy's. As far as the boss can tell, the kid has everything to recommend him: brains, rapidly growing knowledge, youth, and that certain edge. His productivity is rising almost as his employer watches. In other words, he gets—and probably deserves—the biggest raise. His salary will be elevated to the point that it's almost impossible for him to leave.

The boss admires Jane Q. Colgrad, but hers is a different situation. She's a settled company lady now. She isn't really 100 percent informed on all the latest developments. She'll get some kind of raise, but she need not be given a huge amount to make sure that she stays—and she won't be.

Note well that this sad turn of events didn't have to happen for Jane. She could have said, "Well, whatever there is to learn about the new field, I'll learn it." But she didn't do that. Instead, she rested on her laurels and seniority and let someone else build up his position and productivity through knowledge of what's state-of-the-art. The understandable wish of the slightly older employee to take it easy, the natural belief that some rest period is deserved, kept her from staying on the front lines.

Jane Q. Colgrad in this tale is a proxy both for unmarried women who have never left the labor force, as well as for married men. These two groups have similar income-curve prognoses, for the simple reason that they leave the labor force rarely, if at all.

Therefore, they get all the benefits possible from a long term of unbroken service in the field.

Maternity Leave

The married woman typically suffers from all the bad effects of age: obsolescence of knowledge, lack of the best contacts, failure to acquire new expertise, and loss of premium for youth. In addition, she often gets the negative effects of leaving the labor force altogether for a time. This means she misses the seniority payoffs that are a large part of the benefit of continual service.

Even the most career-minded mother is required by the laws of nature and medicine to take *some* time off when a baby arrives. Many employees with a year of service under their belts at larger organizations can take 12 weeks' unpaid leave under the provisions of the Family and Medical Leave Act; some progressive companies may even offer more generous terms. However, if the family decides that it's best for Mother to stay home and raise the kid(s), it will without question negatively impact her income. The sole exception would be for a low-income family where the mother earns minimum wage. In such a case, she's better off not working at all, because the resulting increase in the family's income is more than canceled out by reducing eligibility for various federal income-transfer programs.

(We're indebted to Jagadeesh Gokhale, Laurence Kotlikoff, and the National Center for Policy Analysis for the insight that, due to the incredibly intricate and complicated nature of taxes and subsidies in the United States today, there's an extremely high effective net tax on the second earner in a working couple. If a husband earns $60,000 and his wife makes $30,000, about half of her income will end up going to taxes. This roughly 50 percent tax rate is surprisingly robust as a rule of thumb, even assuming various possible changes in the tax code and across varying family income levels. In this particular instance, if the family plans for her to pay more than $15,000 per year for child care, they might be better off in the long run if Mom stays home. Of course, there are trade-offs.

If the marriage ends in divorce, or the husband loses his job, the wife's independent income stream would come in handy.)

We can also look at all this from the standpoint of the employer. He pays the bills, so his views definitely have to be taken into account. He sees Jean Q. Valleywife, who has been a good employee of his company for ten years. She is, let us say, a sales representative. She's always been one of the boys, getting at least as big a raise as any of them, and the boss has prided himself on this fact.

Now, at the age of 30, Jean Q. Valleywife decides to have a baby and stay home with the infant. When she returns to work after a hiatus of two years, a lot of things have happened in her business. She has to study night and day to learn all the new developments, which isn't easy, because she also has to stay up large parts of the night with her toddler. Jean tries gamely, but when the big buyers come to her showroom, it's clear that she doesn't grasp the new technology as well as the boys in the office.

Not only that, but while Jean was out with the baby (again, a highly important and necessary act for her and for society), there were buyouts and restructuring, and the personnel at the major industry players changed. A lot of these people are completely new to Jean. They have no experience of going out drinking with her after work, or knowing how she fit in before. All this translates into one depressing fact: When it comes time for the raises and bonuses to arrive, Jean's is far smaller than the ones her male colleagues boast about.

This disappointment, compounded over the next two years by yet another minuscule pay increase, leads Jean Q. Valleywife to decide that maybe she should have another baby. Her employer is fond of her, but when she wants to come back—again—there's simply no way that he can fit someone in laterally with his sales force. So she has to find another job. Counting the effects of inflation and the lack of a bonus, Jean's new position pays only about half of what the first one did.

Although the situation of Jean Q. Valleywife is unusually stark, the basic facts are unarguable: Married women who leave the labor force even sporadically have drastically lower rates of income increase than men and women who don't take time off. Usually, the effect is a lower rate of growth rather than an actual drop in salary, but that in itself is a shock in a society accustomed to constantly rising real incomes.

Summary and Conclusion

The peak years of earnings growth go on and on—and then suddenly, they end. The fact is that your income will grow thereafter, but there are a couple of things to keep in mind:

- Your pay will go up much more slowly than it did in previous years.

- If you want to buck the trend, it will take an enormous effort to maintain the same level of earnings growth as when you were younger.

These facts should motivate you to make the adjustments that will keep income, spending, and saving in line, which should be the goal of any man or woman who craves an orderly financial life.

People often get their first opportunity to cope with the collision of a decelerating income with a rising need for money in a familiar context: sending their children off to college. Stay tuned. . . .

◪ ◥ ◪

CHAPTER 14

IN YOUR 40s

Life is so charged with events that every decade is a time of transition. You've seen that the thirties are no picnic in this regard. But the decade of your 40s is so heavily freighted a transition in terms of youth, age, and money growth and decline that it's a particularly acute time.

Let's start with the big picture: Your income is no longer rising much in real terms, as shown in Figure 14.1.

Figure 14.1: Inflation-Adjusted Income in Your 40s

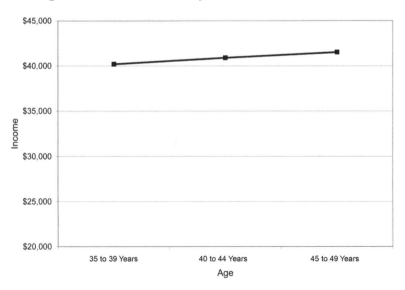

Colliding with this immutable force is an irresistible object: The 40s (and increasingly, the 50s) are the decade in which most American married couples send their children off to college, if they're going to send them at all. This means a genuine shock to all but the most gilded pocketbooks. We have to consider just how much of a jolt this can and will be financially, how a sensible person should look at higher education, who owns it, what it's worth, and why the economic necessities of the 40s make it imperative for most people to place the burden of that cost where the benefits will also go.

College Is Expensive

Table 14.1 shows the average costs of sending a child to one year of college recently (in 2004), courtesy of the College Board:

Table 14.1: U.S. College Costs 2004–2005		
	Public College	**Private College**
Tuition & Fees	$5,132	$20,082
Room & Board	$6,222	$7,434
Books & Supplies	$853	$870
Transportation	$774	$671
Other Expenses	$1,659	$1,238
Total	**$14,640**	**$30,295**

Let us emphasize two words in the sentence above: *average* and *recently.* The word *average* is important because your son or daughter will want to go to a particular school, and costs vary widely. For example, if she goes to Princeton, tuition is $33,000 all by itself.

We underscore *recently* because college costs have been rising steeply. Since 1980, they've gone up two to three times as much as the consumer price index (CPI). By way of pointed comparison, your income in your 40s is likely to be rising pretty much in lockstep with the CPI. For the last five years, college costs have risen about 5 percent per year.

Why are these fees so out of control? The answer is easy to see. While colleges may be competitive to get into, they don't compete among themselves in any meaningful sense except in athletics. They have no quantitative goals regarding the education of their students and therefore no program evaluation to measure whether they're being successful in meeting their goals. There's a proliferation of ancillary staff and services that contribute nothing to the education of students. Majors abound in hundreds of areas without respect to any marketplace for graduates in those fields.

There are no competence-based standards for graduation that would offer future employers any reason to take college diplomas seriously, although they still do. College faculty work very part-time, and campuses are in full use for only a couple of semesters a year. Given the lackadaisical pace, it's not surprising to learn that it increasingly takes five years to complete a four-year degree.

According to survey funded by the Pew Charitable Trusts, only one-third of students at four-year colleges and universities are skilled enough at math to balance a checkbook. Only 38 percent were proficient enough to read and understand a basic newspaper article. In short, despite the astronomical expense, college education is something of a scam in many cases. The schools are models of inefficiency and a perfect breeding ground for malcontents of every description—which are exactly what you find if you tour campuses today.

Nevertheless, Americans love to go to college; 17.1 million did so in 2004, according to the National Center for Education Statistics. In this country, almost two-thirds of high-school graduates will enter an institute of higher learning (although half will drop out before earning even ten credits). The prospect of sending a child to college today reminds us of Adam Smith's verdict on the common practice in his day of sending a young man off on a grand tour of Europe in order to broaden his mind:

> . . . he commonly returns home more conceited, more unprincipled, more dissipated, and more incapable of any serious application either to study or to business than he could well have become in so short a time had he lived at home. . . . by spending in the

139

most frivolous dissipation the most precious years of his life, at a distance from the inspection and control of his parents and relations, every useful habit which the earlier parts of his education might have had some tendency to form in him, instead of being riveted and confirmed, is almost necessarily either weakened or effaced. (Book V, *The Wealth of Nations*)

In spite of all the foregoing, we're forced to recommend college for those who will complete it, if only for the career advantage its diploma bestows. The game may sometimes be crooked, but it's the only one in town.

College Costs Come at a Horrible Time

The expenditures of a typical middle-class family on education for one child in a public school of higher education will generally exceed its total expenditures on food, transportation, and recreation for the entire family. They'll come close to equaling total expenditures for shelter and be very nearly as large as all state and federal tax costs. In other words, they're stupendous.

Unfortunately, these expenses often come at a time of slow growth in real income, which makes them especially burdensome. All the reasons that slowed down earnings growth in the late 30s begin to bite even harder in the 40s. The premium for youth is now gone, and the increments of knowledge that used to be so valuable are now frequently of trivial importance. Imagine just how much you learn about doing a typical job on the 5th day as compared with the 1,500th day. On the former, you learn crucial data about how to work; on the latter, it's just more of the same. Not only that, but a lot of what you've learned is obsolete by now. The rules of the game change; there are new players and products, and even entirely different approaches to the field.

All of this changes the earnings curve on which you now find yourself. Instead of the glorious pace at which you were rocketing upward, raises now just keep you even with inflation. The sad fact is that by the time most workers are in their 40s, they're no longer red-hot commodities in the job market. They may be perfectly wonderful workers, good parents, loyal friends, and devoted members of the Kiwanis—but they just aren't in demand the way that 30-year-olds are.

Employers want the young and the hustlers. Increasingly, this bias is reinforced by insurance costs, since young people are healthier and much cheaper to insure than those who are middle-aged and older. While the numbers and the facts behind them are averages, fortysomethings face a real-life problem in terms of the lack of a youth premium, the obsolescence of their knowledge base, and increased competition from new workers.

While pay increases slow down drastically in the 40s, most people also have less need for cash (assuming they've been keeping up with the funding of their retirement accounts). The down payment for a home has usually been made several years before the 40th birthday of the family's primary breadwinner. Inflation and the growth of earnings have tamed the monthly payments. Husband and wife have adjusted to whatever kind of cars they really want, in the sense that they know now that everything they buy costs something—that is, they have what they can afford to buy and are willing to pay for. True, the kiddies cost more year by year as they go through public or private high school. But these expenses are manageable in light of the growing family income.

In other words, everything is going swimmingly until college comes along, causing a dramatic, spectacularly painful spike in spending. It's as if the family were cruising in a minivan down the highway of life, when suddenly they come to a pothole about 20 feet deep and 50 feet in diameter. It's a big problem, and solving it requires reconceptualizing the whole idea of college.

What Is a College Education?

Imagine that your daughter wants to buy a piece of rental property. The kid is shrewd, and she figures that owning it will make her life a lot easier in years to come. After all, that real estate will come in handy, pouring in rents that rise in worth year after year as the neighborhood becomes more valuable. She figures that whatever she can add to the pot by working will be nice, but that income property will really do wonders for her budget.

Or, imagine that your son wants to have a handsome new diesel tractor-trailer rig, costing about $100,000, as a present for his 18th birthday. The child figures that he can rent it out to a driver, collect a portion of the haulage fees, and make a good addition to his living doing it. He knows that the income will pad his earnings from whatever job he undertakes.

Would you feel comfortable giving your child a piece of investment machinery, a capital good, that costs you as much as a couple of years of your salary? Would you feel that it was your duty as a parent to provide an income property that sets you back six figures?

Probably that idea strikes you as astonishing and, more than that, as something you'd never do. You probably can't imagine that it would be your bounden duty to give such a huge capital asset to your son or daughter, something producing income that would flow exclusively to the child, at a time when buying such a gift would wreak havoc upon your own financial life.

Yet that's what a huge number of parents do by paying for their children's higher education. A degree is (at most) an earning asset for the kids, much like the piece of real estate or the tractor-trailer rig. To see just how major a capital asset it will turn out to be—and to think further about who should pay for it—we'll look at the history of lifetime payoff from college.

How Much Is a College Education Worth?

Once upon a time, higher education represented a truly immense difference for its owner compared with a man or woman who only completed high school. Before World War II, a man with a college degree might confidently expect to earn over his lifetime three times more than a man without one. Of course, there were all kinds of tricks involved in that calculation, such as the much smaller pool of college graduates, the fact that many of these individuals were already rich and well connected, and the fact that right after World War II there was a period of almost unprecedented economic growth and therefore a shortage of well-trained workers. Still, as late as 1965, the extra education meant earnings of approximately twice as much as those without that advantage.

But even in 2003, a college graduate could expect to make about 1.7 times as much as a high-school grad over his or her lifetime. (See figure 2.1 on page 13.) There are flaws in the comparison of 2003 and 1941, such as the vastly larger pool of college graduates, implying a lowering of average ability within that pool. But in plain English, that college education is going to be worth a huge amount of money to your offspring. It's like starting them out with a cushy inheritance or trust fund purchased with the blood, toil, tears, and sweat of Mom and Dad.

Is it fair, decent, or even sensible for the old and tired to bleed for the young and vigorous? Certainly not. Since earnings increases will be far smaller in years to come, making Mom and Dad shell out for this tuition doesn't make sense.

143

Make the Kids Pay

The owner of the college-generated lifetime stream of income should pay for it. Unless parents are so well-to-do that they won't miss $15,000 to $30,000 or more per child every year, unless they're so guilt-ridden that they feel they owe a lot of suffering and an impoverished old age to themselves in return for the kids' love and kisses (which they may never get anyway), they should let Junior and Sis finance college themselves.

There are many ways that the younger set can pay for their college education. There are scholarships, work-study programs, and deferred-tuition plans. There are loans handed out by the federal government (including Stafford, Signature, Perkins, and Community College), loans offered by state governments, grants of a hundred different descriptions offered by the federal government, scholarships of every kind, and jobs checking out library books that allow the kids to study while they earn a small living.

All of these are resources for allowing a child to acquire his or her college education with the active help and subsidization of the state and its citizens. Frank Knight, one of the great geniuses in the field of economics, said that a key to success for young people was "Take advantage of all subsidies."

After the huge subsidy this country gives for housing (which we discussed in Chapter 6), its next largest is for education. The government takes tens of billions of dollars away from bricklayers, field hands assembly-line workers, dentists, doctors, and lawyers each year to create gifts for young men and women who want to go to college. These presents take the form of outright grants, subsidized low-interest-rate loans, subsidized jobs, and gifts and loans to the higher-education institutions. There's absolutely no reason why your family shouldn't take advantage of them. You've probably paid plenty of taxes in your time, so you might as well pick up some of the money that our politicians have redistributed back to the citizenry in exchange for votes.

Beyond that, even if your child can't qualify for a government gift, there are other ways for him or her to pay for college. Here's a thought: How about getting a job? Investigate scholarships based upon merit or the specialization of the student. There are loans from financial institutions that are specially geared for the unique circumstances of college students, allowing them a long period before they must repay any of the funds and then stretching out the payments over a number of years.

There are also loans from potential employers that are automatically repaid by the graduate working for that company. The first and most well known of such employers is the U.S. Department of Defense, but there are others as well, generally large corporations with a need for certain kinds of specialists. If worst comes to worst, there are loans from well-to-do family members, which should always be entered into in the solemn spirit that they will really and truly be repaid.

However these options are combined, the bottom line is that the student should pay for the education.

Yes, if Mom and Dad are multimillionaires, they can handle the cost without missing a beat. But for most parents who see their income stagnating, there's nothing to argue that children should do anything but finance their own education. Let the owner of the asset pay for it.

Just as compelling, the student will then be repaying the loans out of an income stream which is rising dramatically, instead of forcing poor old Ma and Pa to funnel funds from earnings that are flatlining. Of course, the parents will have an income stream far larger than Junior when he first gets out of school, but they'll also have much greater expenses and possibly other dependents still in secondary school. Ma and Pa have scarce dollars in the future and a gaping retirement to fund; the kids have plentiful income ahead.

Will making children pay for their own capital goods (college education) keep them from getting good grades in school? No. There's no evidence available from the financial-aid officers to suggest that the marks of students receiving assistance are lower than those who aren't receiving help. More interesting, several of these officials told us that kids who work part-time through college tend to be more studious and get *better* grades than those receiving all their support from home. This isn't really surprising, since we expect a student who knows what education costs in terms of sweat to treasure it more than someone who just deposits a series of checks from Mom and Dad each semester. It's human nature to value things more highly that we have to work to acquire.

145

But what about the idea that Junior and Sis are not only getting knowledge at college but are also having fun and living it up in a way that their poor old parents weren't able to in their poverty-stricken youth? Shouldn't the grown-ups feel good about giving their kids a four-year party when they, the parents, had to work at the dry-cleaning shop all week long when they were in their early 20s?

The answer is that such a line of argument has nothing to do with economics. If there are compelling psychological reasons for parents to stretch themselves thin financially so that Junior and Sis can live it up, it has nothing to do with lifetime earnings and spending. If Mom and Dad really believe that they're doing something noble by depriving themselves so that their kids can stay out all night drinking in Nassau during spring vacation, that has little to do with rational thought.

College education is a fine thing, especially one that passes on something of value from Western civilization. But whatever is or isn't being learned, it will be a capital expenditure for most people: money spent to produce income. Unless parents can spare the cash without missing it, they should make Junior and Sis pay for as much of that capital good as possible. Not only is this the most rational way to look at the process, it's also the method that will help develop the best appreciation of college (and education in general) in the minds of students.

Interest, School, and the Future

Let's bring a certain fine point to the discussion by considering the question of funding the children's college education alongside another big-ticket item on the list: providing for your own retirement. You might love nothing more than to pay for your kids to go to school, just as you might adore driving a Bentley. The question is, of course: Can you afford it?

If you're 45 years old and already have at least three years of your family's annual salary in untouchable investment accounts dedicated solely to retirement, then you can consider paying for some of your children's college. This projection, like all others, make a number of assumptions, but they're probably reasonable.

Perhaps you delayed having children until later so that now you're 55 years old. In that case, you want to have six years' salary in the bank before helping them out with school (and this assumes that you'll be continuing to make uninterrupted deposits to your retirement accounts).

If you don't have these amounts in dedicated retirement savings, you can't afford to spend money on your children's college education. It's cash you don't have. You'll just be buying yourself a ticket to the poorhouse (or a ticket for your spouse—usually the wife, after the husband is gone). There's nothing noble about feeling like a big shot by giving your kids a free ride now at the expense of condemning your wife to poverty later.

146

The Lifetime Impact of College Expenses

We plugged Junior and Sis's college costs into ESPlanner and took them for a spin. We made the usual assumptions and variations:

- The couple bought their home at age 35.

- They had zero, one, or two children.

- All the kids attended average low-cost private (that is, religious-oriented) schools for primary and secondary education.

- The kids went to an average-priced public college, a private college, or none at all.

The upshot of all these variations is seen in Figure 14.2, which shows the average numbers of dollars available for consumption for each of these hypothetical families (in constant dollars) from when the parents are age 31 and first start saving to have a house and kids (if applicable) until the year both Mom and Dad retire at age 66. Dollars available for consumption are those left after they've paid for housing, taxes, education, retirement savings, and insurance.

Figure 14.2: Impact of College Expenses on Average Annual Dollars Available for Consumption by Median Income Families

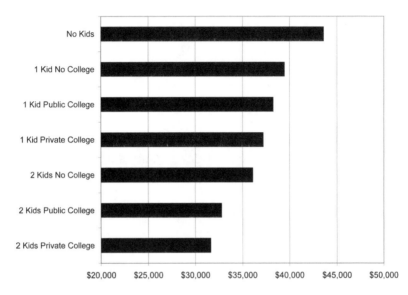

Figure 14.2 puts into relief the relative cost of having children and putting them through college. If anything, it understates the impact that paying for education has on a family, because these sums end up being divided among all family members in the household: Mom, Dad, Sis, and Junior. If it's just Mom, Dad, and Sis, there's one less mouth to feed. If it's just Mom and Dad, they can lavish all those consumption dollars on themselves alone.

529 Plans

If you choose to put money aside in advance to pay for your children's college educations, you should consider a 529 plan, so called because they floated up like Venus on a clamshell from Section 529 of the Internal Revenue Code. They're operated at the state level and run with exactly the degree of incompetence that you'd expect. The basic idea is that your money is invested in mutual funds in a tax-deferred wrapper, and then can be pulled out tax-free years later to send Junior to State U, so long as the funds are used for legitimate college expenses (beer doesn't count). These plans vary widely in quality from state to state, and you'll have to look carefully at what's available where you live.

In some states, you can deduct your contribution from your income for the purposes of calculating your state income tax. If your state is one of these, you'll want to pay special attention to the rest of the plan's provisions.

The next thing to watch is fees, which we must warn you are almost impossible to track down. The reason is that they're often unconscionably high. The mutual fund companies have done a great job selling the plans to clueless government functionaries as a way for them to swell the state coffers under the fig leaf of providing a valuable service to citizens.

Some of these plans offer prepaid tuition at today's rates to schools within your state; others do the same for a list of subscribing private colleges (but note that Junior still needs to gain admittance to these schools). Still others let you use the tax-deferred funds to pay for school anywhere (but at tomorrow's rates). This latter group seems like the best ticket to us, since we like to keep our options open, but they may be wrong for you.

Now for the good news: If you don't like your state's plan, you can always take your money to some other state's plan that you like better. Of course, this forfeits any up-front tax deduction, which makes it a grievous move in those states where such an incentive is offered, but it would still preserve the tax deferral. We'll provide a link to a site summarizing the provisions of these various state plans on our Website (**www.stein-demuth.com**), but in the meantime we'll cut to the chase and tell you the two 529 plans that we like best: Nevada's and Utah's. Both of these offer access to low-expense Vanguard index funds without too hefty a surcharge tacked on by the state for allowing you the privilege of parking your money with them.

Other Expenses: Declining

After you hit middle age, expenditures in most major categories start to decline year by year. For example, the totals spent on food at home and in restaurants decline after 45. The percentage spent on housing decreases slightly, as does the percentage going to household operations. There are tiny increases in the amounts spent on clothing and transportation, but overall, household spending generally shrinks little by little in most areas.

This raises a fairly obvious question: If expenditures are falling in all of those categories, where's the money going? Not surprisingly, it's moving to insurance, medical expenses, retirement savings, and all the other preparations for old age. Additionally, it's going into another worthy category: recreation.

For most families with adults in their 30s, life is too hectic to enjoy many leisure activities. There are the pressures of getting ahead on the job, bringing up babies, and getting divorced and remarried. There are also the sudden needs of replacing a spouse's lost income (in the case of divorce) and making certain that the children are finding their way in the world.

People don't take much time off for fun and games while they're having their period of greatest income growth. The reason for this is that they're doing the key things for young families: replacing their generation and improving their standard of living. Neither of those is a part-time job, nor do they allow much time for travel or other recreation.

You can hardly expect to see Mont-Saint-Michel and Chartres while you're working long hours trying to become vice president of sales. You don't collect brass rubbings in Scotland while you're awaiting word from the pediatrician about whether or not Sis has the measles. You can't count on becoming a ten-handicap golfer while you're working every Saturday to learn options strategies.

But in your 40s, when career path and home life have stabilized somewhat, the time for recreation is at hand. You have the advantage of being young enough to enjoy the strenuous pace of athletics and travel, as you did when you were in your 20s, along with the professional and familial stability to do so with some peace of mind.

CHAPTER 15

INVESTING, 40s-STYLE

L et's check in on your investments, shall we? The cash reserves sitting in your money market fund are probably fine at where they were set in your 30s, unless you've tapped into them for some reason and need to replenish them. The big idea is to have enough to cover standard family events (sudden trips, medical bills, or a new roof or transmission) or three to six months of income, depending on how secure your job(s) are.

Your tax-deferred retirement accounts need to be rejiggered at this point to reflect the fact that there are fewer years remaining from today until the day you plan to retire. You have less time to make up for any drastic market correction, and by now you have far more money at stake, so you need to nudge your portfolio in a more conservative direction. It's time to check into the classic 60 percent equity/40 percent fixed income portfolio, as shown in Figure 15.1.

Figure 15.1: 40s Asset Allocation

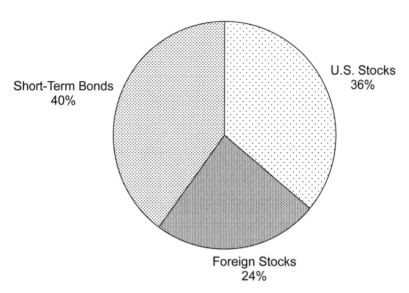

Short-Term Bonds
40%

U.S. Stocks
36%

Foreign Stocks
24%

As before, the options within your 401(k) plan will probably have to approximate the ideal shown here: 36 percent total U.S. stock market, 24 percent total foreign stock market, and 40 percent short-term bonds. Try to get as close to this as you can. We've kept the ratio of domestic to foreign stocks constant and simply added more short-term bonds as ballast. If you deferred contributing to these accounts for a while in order to make the down payment on your house or put your children through private school, now would be a great time to get back to topping them off religiously.

Consult Table 15.1 to see whether your savings are on track. We're assuming that this money is being saved in a tax-deferred retirement account, or, to the extent that it's being held in taxable accounts, you're paying the taxes on the capital gains and dividends yourself without drawing on the principal. We're also assuming that you can live on 84 percent of your preretirement income after you stop working at age 70 (adjusted for the fact that you no longer need to save for retirement after you've retired).

Table 15.1: Recommended Savings Rates as % of Current Salary for Constant Pre- & Post-Retirement Standard of Living

If You Have in Savings:	You Should Save:		
	Age 40	Age 45	Age 50
No Retirement Savings	20%	28%	35%
Savings = 1 Year's Salary	12%	21%	30%
Savings = 2 Years' Salary	5%	13%	26%
Savings = 3 Years' Salary	0%	5%	17%
Savings = 4 Years' Salary	0%	0%	8%
Savings = 5 Years' Salary	0%	0%	0%

Notice how it's now karma time for those without adequate funds already set aside. The stringency of the required savings rates for the shorter period ahead to accumulate a nest egg means that these folks may not be able to retire on 84 percent of their preretirement salary (which some researchers estimate would give them the same standard of living overall that their salary gave them while they were still working).

However, it makes little sense for a 50-year-old with zero savings to squirrel away 45 percent of his salary for 20 years in order to have a jump in income when he retires on 84 percent of his prior salary. This isn't income smoothing. Instead, the best course would be to balance his preretirement savings against his postretirement income in order to maintain the same standard of living from today onward, even if that requires a step down from what his standard of living would have been if he'd accumulated more savings earlier. Unfortunately, that train has already left the station, so he has to make the best of it given the choices he has now. You'll just have to live on less now *and* in the future if you weren't prudent when you were young.

The rates prescribed in Table 15.1 take the possibility of this reduced lifestyle into account. The more you have today, the less you have to set aside going forward, and the more money you'll be able to withdraw after you retire. Where the prescribed savings rate is greater than 16 percent, this usually implies that there will be some step down in lifestyle overall. The longer you wait to begin squirreling away your cash, the bigger this step down will be. That's the moral of Table 15.1.

Table 15.2 shows whether your nest egg is of a size that, with further contributions, will likely fund your retirement at your highest possible preretirement standard of living.

Table 15.2: Are Your Retirement Savings on Track? Multiple of Current Salary You Ideally Have in Savings	
Age	Retirement Savings
40	2
45	3
50	4

At age 45, every dollar you can save toward your retirement is worth about two dollars saved at age 55. If you have difficulty finding that dollar today, we assure you that it won't be any easier to find two of them when you're ten years older.

If you find yourself on the borderline, wondering whether or not you're going to make it, remember that we're assuming that your retirement will be entirely self-funded, with not a penny coming in from a pension, Social Security, or an inheritance. If you think that you'll be getting something from these, then you won't need to provide as much yourself. This would be a good time to get the ESPlanner software and spend some time entering the details of your personal situation, while you have plenty of opportunity to take corrective action. If you wait a decade to take a searching and fearless inventory of your financial life and discover that you've guessed wrong, you'll have fewer and less pleasant options available to rectify the situation at that point.

In your 20s and 30s, when you were saving for the down payment for your house or for having children, we recommended that you put your cash into a single, balanced, low-expense mutual fund, such as those shown in Table 4.1 (see page 44). This still isn't a terrible idea, especially if you're contemplating some major expense in the intermediate, indeterminate future, such as the down payment for a second home, the purchase of a boat, or paying for a daughter's wedding. But if your goals are longer term (retirement, leaving money to your heirs), you can probably do better.

Savings Outside of Retirement Accounts

If you've been extremely fortunate or industrious, it's entirely possible that you're beginning to accumulate savings beyond what it takes to fund your cash reserves and retirement accounts. There will be no shortage of people who are lined up to take the responsibility for handling this money off your hands. They'll try to make you feel like a VIP if you work with them. Nevertheless, in most cases you'll do better if you politely eschew their services and invest the money yourself, following a low-expense, tax-efficient, indexing strategy.

What's this? Why, precisely the same course we recommend for your retirement accounts: 36 percent total U.S. stock market, 24 percent total international stock market, and 40 percent short-term bonds. What's good for the goose is good for the gander, with one exception: If you're earning enough to have a taxable investment account, you undoubtedly will do better if, instead of owning a taxable bond fund, you buy a municipal bond fund instead. If you live in a high-tax state (you'll know if you do), you'll do better still if you own bonds from your own backyard, where the income will be exempt from state taxes as well. We wouldn't own long-term bonds, since these tend to be quite volatile, but short- or even intermediate-term municipal bonds should be fine.

If you want to be really clever, you can park all your bonds in your tax-deferred accounts and all your stocks in your taxable accounts, provided you keep your total holdings allocated at the same 60/40 ratio of stocks to bonds.

But for now, let's not be quite that smart. Let's just be smarter than almost every other investor your authors have ever met and open an account at a low-expense provider like Vanguard or Fidelity. Tables 15.3 and 15.4 show how we'd allocate a taxable account at either of these companies.

Table 15.3 Vanguard Taxable Account

Fund	Ticker	Allocation	Expense Ratio
Vanguard Total Stock Market Index	VTSMX	36%	0.19
Vanguard Total International Stock Index	VGTSX	24%	0.31
Vanguard Limited-Term Tax Exempt Bond	VMLTX	40%	0.16

Table 15.4 Fidelity Taxable Account

Fund	Ticker	Allocation	Expense Ratio
Fidelity Spartan Total Stock Market Index	FSTMX	36%	0.10
Fidelity Spartan International Index	FSIIX	24%	0.10
Fidelity Short-Intermediate Muni Income	FSTFX	40%	0.47

Are more sophisticated portfolios possible? Undoubtedly. But the ones we recommend will be hard to beat—especially over time, after account expenses and taxes are taken into account, and on a risk-adjusted basis. Instead of staying up late at night worrying about how you might tweak that last 10th of a percent out of your investments, you'll be better off simply indexing them and going to bed.

Invest your money in the markets and keep it there. Don't get fancy—just rebalance the account every few years or when you're adding new money. Other than to confirm that there are no mistakes, checking your brokerage statement once a quarter or even once a year is plenty. Let other people brag about how hot their stocks are. This means they made $500 (except they forgot to mention the $500 they lost last year.) Put your time and energy to better use, such as by reading a good book or walking your dog.

◢◣◢

CHAPTER 16

SINGLE AND 40

Y ou might think that the man or woman who's single, without dependents, and making a decent living would enjoy the best of all possible financial worlds. You might think that, but you would be wrong.

The truth is that a single person in his 40s faces difficult prospects. Yes, a single man who earns as much as his married neighbor and has no dependents will have more money to spend on himself. And also, yes, a single woman who makes as much as the combined Mom and Dad across the hall will have far more money to spend on herself than they do.

But this is usually not the case. Figure 16.1 shows the median income curve of all married people versus that of males and females who live alone. The data is from the U.S. Census Bureau's 2005 Annual Social and Economic Survey. Unlike our previous graphs, these aren't necessarily the incomes of people who worked full-time year round; it's all people who worked during that 12-month period, even if their employment was sporadic. Nevertheless, it's enough to give a single person pause.

Figure 16.1: Inflation-Adjusted Income: Single vs. Married

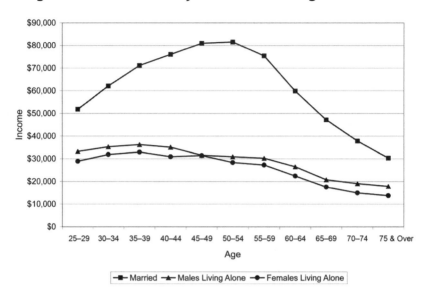

The main reason why the income of single people rose far less rapidly than that of those who are married was that the former left and reentered the labor force more frequently than the latter. They failed to acquire the seniority that the espoused breadwinner acquired. To put it even more starkly, while the married man is at the grindstone year after year, piling up knowledge and connections while trying to make the mortgage payment, the single mother is at home changing diapers and forgetting what she knew about her last job. And the never-married man is changing jobs rapidly and frittering away his seniority and connections.

That crude schematic may not in fact be exactly what happens, but it's close enough to what goes on in the minds of many employers when they think about how much to pay single men or women versus married ones. The employer also has another consideration: He may feel that because married people, usually with children, have those mouths to feed at home, he ought to pay them more money than a single person with only a cat, a Tivo, and an answering machine waiting in the condo. But even here, the employer doesn't pay the married employee strictly out of the goodness of his heart. The employer offers more because he thinks that he has to in order to compete with other companies.

Whatever the reasons, the income of unmarried men and women as a group virtually stops rising by the time they're in their 40s.

Divorce, Realistic Style

This lack of income growth has a staggering impact upon all working fortysomethings who are single, but it has the most devastating and disabling effect upon one particular subcategory: the man or woman who's getting divorced, still having duties to the old family, and possibly about to undertake responsibilities to a new one.

Look at it carefully. If a young man, say around age 30, has a wife and two small children, then gets divorced and starts a new family, he can look forward to rapidly rising real income for at least ten years. He can confidently expect to pay the alimony and the child support out of this rising income stream.

But if a man of 45 gets divorced, he may still have to pay child support and alimony, as a woman may in the same situation. But he can't count on drawing from an ever-growing pot of money. Income is rising slowly, if at all, in inflation-adjusted terms. The new dollars that once floated in as if by magic are now slowed down to a trickle.

If a 45-year-old man leaves his family and starts to live either as a bachelor or with a new family, he can't and shouldn't expect that the going will be easy. Whether counted as a married man or as a single person with the attendant stable income, his salary is still rising so slowly that he can't expect automatically to be able to support two families, or even one family and one other individual (such as his new girlfriend), on the scale that he might have expected.

A staple of drama is the middle-aged man who leaves his middle-aged wife for a young woman. On TV and in books, they live in glamorous seaside condos with sports cars and weekend getaways to Cabo San Lucas. In fact, the old husband and the new wife (or girlfriend) can be expected to be on a short tether, financially.

This fact, unappreciated by most middle-aged divorced men, gradually gets brought to their attention. When it finally hits home

159

that there isn't enough money for the old family plus the *new* woman or family, you can guess who and what gets cut out—certainly not the new girlfriend, and not the rejuvenated lifestyle.

All too often, it's the first family, including the children, who get the boot. The standard way that divorced men are tempted to cope with the problem of income rising very slowly while expenditures shoot up at a crisis rate is to stop paying alimony and child support in a responsible way. This has powerful implications for everyone involved. While legal enforcement of these payments has become more aggressive over the years, it's hardly a pleasant or trouble-free process.

The man contemplating divorce should and must bear in mind that his life afterward won't be one long round of blonde showgirls and visits home to dazzle the kiddies with lavish gifts. He'll probably enter a period of severe economic privation without any foreseeable end point. The myth is a glamorous life; the fact is riding the bus.

160

For the midlife wife facing a divorce, a good, healthy dose of reality is also in order. Despite all the promises, court orders, and contracts, there's every likelihood that the ex-husband either won't pay the alimony and child support, or may do so only after prolonged and contentious legal battles on her part. This means that the wife, for her sake and that of the children, should try to get her hands on tangible property in the here and now, rather than pieces of paper describing the future. The wife should and must get as much as she possibly can of any jointly owned real property, especially income-producing real property and assets such as stocks, bonds, or CDs. Owning the things she'll need in the future—such as a home and a stream of income—will be crucial.

The cast-off wife and children (sometimes the cast-off husband and children) will be far happier and better off if they have sources of money that aren't dependent upon the ex-spouse's financial course. Even if the ex-husband, for example, is a genuinely wonderful man—founder of the local PTA, blood donor every two weeks, scratch golfer, and decorated veteran of Iraq—he'll still come under pressure to stop sending those support payments as his expenses inevitably rise and his income stops growing.

To be smart about it, the wife who sees her 40-ish husband drifting out the door will take the cash, house, and financial assets right now. She should let her husband make well-intentioned promises of support to himself or his new friend. For her part, the ex-wife should place heavy emphasis on the here-and-now, on assets she can hold in her hand or live or ride around in.

Sharing the Burden, Family Style

We've already mentioned that over 9 percent of all U.S. families with children are headed by single moms. There are a great many single and/or divorced men and women in their 40s whose incomes have virtually stopped increasing while their children are growing, and who need more money than ever before. This is one of the true financial crises of American life.

Wherever possible, these children of divorce have to be converted into assets. In this society, there's an enormous (and still-growing) number of jobs that require teenage labor. If you have teenagers, they can fill that need and help defray some of their expenses. Car parkers, baggers at grocery stores, dog walkers, baby-sitters, and messengers are all earning less than a brain surgeon, but a great deal more than zero. Unless you have so much money that you don't know what to do, you should enlist your kids' help in keeping the financial ship afloat.

Will this harm your children? Absolutely not. It stands to reason that a 16-year-old who works a few hours after school three days a week sweeping up at a shop so that Mom can keep the wolf from the door will feel a lot better about himself than a kid who's hanging around the mall. Giving children a chance to earn money gives them the opportunity to garner some self-respect—and allows the parent a chance to catch his or her financial breath.

161

A Bad Time for Borrowing

Be wary of borrowing in this decade of your life. There's an axiom stating that you should always try to borrow valuable dollars and repay them with cheap ones. This means, for example, that you should get loans when you're broke and in medical school, because each dollar you receive then is worth a lot to you. You repay the money when you have your own clinic and need the tax write-off.

A second example is that it's better to borrow when there's high inflation, because it will shower you with dollars that are worth less down the road, and you can use those worth-less funds to repay your loans.

By the exact same token, you should avoid borrowing valuable dollars and paying them back with even more valuable ones. This means that you shouldn't take out loans and have to repay them with money that's harder to come by than what you took out in the first place. Unfortunately, this is precisely the situation in which many 40-ish folks find themselves. They borrow money with the expectation that they can repay it from the ever-growing stream of income that they experienced in their 20s and 30s. Then they discover that the funds aren't forthcoming.

There are some situations—such as medical, housing, and car emergencies—when borrowing is absolutely necessary. But in general, single men and women in their 40s should fight against the temptation. You don't want to repay valuable dollars with cash that comes out of your hide.

Luxury Bracket Creep

There is a notion in this country that families are supposed to live more luxuriously as they grow older. We accept that college students often live like slobs. We expect men and women just out of school and starting work to get by on the cheap, perhaps spending too much on cocktails and clothing. We anticipate that men and women in their 30s might travel abroad and buy a German

162

car. We aren't surprised when individuals and families in their 40s hire decorators for their homes and have tennis courts, swimming pools, or maybe a boat in the water.

The image of older people living more luxuriously is based upon fact and also upon media hype. On television, we watch couples congratulating each other on having started out poor and now owning a chain of stores with annual sales in the tens of millions, and who now give each other matching Rolexes.

The fact is that middle-class couples in their 40s usually *do* live better than their counterparts who are still in their 20s. It seems too obvious to state, but it must be noted: This isn't because the older couples have been alive longer, but rather because they have more money.

Many perfectly fine people get confused and think that persons and families in their 40s automatically accrue luxury goods because of their age, not because they have more wherewithal. But no one automatically gets anything from age except gray or less hair (as your authors can testify). People should acquire goods and services according to what they can afford, not by the number of candles on their birthday cake.

163

If you're a single man or woman in his or her 40s with children, without a large salary, and with your income no longer rapidly growing (maybe not even increasing at all), you have to be alert. Don't think that you can afford a trip to Cannes just because other 40s friends can swing it (or, more likely, have deluded themselves into thinking that they can). If you obligate yourself to spend money that you don't have, you're setting yourself up for sorrow.

If you're a single parent in your 40s, by all that's right and fair you should be entitled to a richer lifestyle. But that doesn't mean that you can have one and still pay the bills. Only a complete fool will throw himself and his children into debt to pay for a life that fits the stereotype for his age but is far beyond his wallet.

Fancy cars, furniture, and vacations are fine for the few who can afford them. For those who pretend that these are within reach, who deceive themselves into thinking they can afford something because other people have done so, nothing but disaster lies ahead. This goes double for single parents. It's incomparably more valuable to set some money aside for family emergencies than to have designer furniture. Real avoidance of financial crises comes from matching your income with your expenditure. For most 40s singles with children, that matchup doesn't permit lifestyle bracket creep.

Lay Down That Housing Burden

The 45-year-old single may say over and over again that he or she wants to be married. But if this person is still unmarried at the age of 45, the likelihood is high that he or she prefers to remain single. This is a "revealed preference" to all parties concerned. Of course, many single, straight 40-year-old women would probably marry George Clooney, if he begged; and many single, straight 40-year-old males would marry Angelina Jolie, if she pouted. But the real-world choices may not be so attractive.

Should this person, then, buy a home? Frankly, at the age of 45, if a single man or woman doesn't yet have a house, it may be that the optimal time for owning has passed. From this stage onward, it might be better to rent. It takes energy to crank up the old Toro and mow the lawn, to rake leaves on crisp fall evenings, and to wait at home for hours for the cable guy to arrive. This is largely a young person's line of work.

If you're single, 40, and still living in rented quarters even though you have no dependents and could afford to own a home, you're almost certainly revealing a preference to rent. At the age of 40 and older, that characteristic starts to harmonize with your economic future.

When men and women were in their 20s and 30s, it made perfect sense for them to undertake paying off a mortgage. At those times when real income was rising so rapidly, the heavy burden of a mortgage was rapidly lightened. But now, when salary growth has crept to a halt, mortgage payments won't automatically be lifted from your shoulders. The shock of large housing costs will remain unpleasant for a good long while, with nothing but inflation to offset them. The difference between the cost of rental and owned housing is still so large that the new total cost of home ownership is almost always a shock.

If you don't need to possess a house outright for some special reason, and if you have only a slight inclination to be a home owner, remember that you can almost always afford to rent in a better neighborhood than you can buy into. Doing so will also free up more of your cash for your investment portfolio, where it might be more productive. If you do buy, arrange for your mortgage to be paid off by the time you plan to retire.

◪ ◪ ◪

CHAPTER 17

In Your 50s

F or a healthy American male, the age of 50 is a milestone in a number of ways. Usually, if he's a family man, his children are well on their way through school and largely out the door. He has attained some measure of success in his work and achieved a sense of security by virtue of saving and investing. He still has a long stretch of time left on this earth. A healthy American male of 50 can reasonably anticipate living another 27 years, but he might stick around for another 50.

It's the same story for the healthy American female, who can anticipate living until she's very close to 80. In other words, she has almost as much of her adult life left ahead of her as she's already lived. This is both a hazard and an opportunity.

This situation is the financial challenge for the American man and woman in their 50s. There are other fiscal problems, but providing for a life span that might dramatically outlast your working years is the key problem of later life.

Flatlining Income

All the factors that made for a gradual flattening of income from the late 30s onward intensify in the 50s, as shown in Figure 17.1.

Figure 17.1: Inflation-Adjusted Income in Your 50s

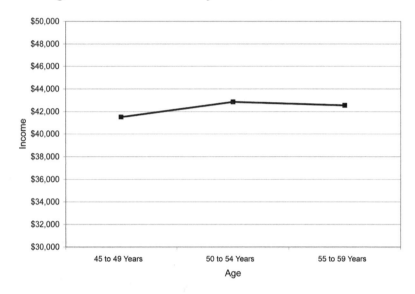

168   This is a depressing development. Men and women in the labor force who are older than 50 are no longer in with the hip young gunslingers of industry. To be sure, their flat-to-declining average income conceals a great deal of movement around the extremes. There will be some men and women who make it their business to stay completely and totally abreast of everything that happens in their fields.

If new technology is introduced, they'll make sure they master it. If the Chinese become a major factor in the market, they'll be poring over *The Wall Street Journal Asia* at all hours of the day and night. If new players come into the business, they'll invite those people to play golf, help them find an apartment or a date, and generally make sure these folks know who their friends are.

But all of this takes a great deal of exertion, and many people would rather do something else with their time. And so at the other end of the spectrum, there will be men and women in their 50s who have reached the point of rapidly falling income. Secretaries get replaced by voice mail and e-mail.

For most intents and purposes, whatever you need now will have to be paid for out of a static pool of income. You're living in a zero-sum universe, which means that new purchases will have to come from eliminating something else. It's vital to adjust consumption in your 50s so that you don't take money out of savings.

Retirement Reality Check

If you haven't been putting aside enough money for your retirement, those new savings will have to come from giving up some other item. If your discipline in setting money aside has been less than rigorous, or if the stock market has been unkind, you may have to save a ridiculous amount of cash today just to reach what will be a very modest standard of living at the time you stop working.

Your best bet is to delay retirement as long as possible and find an area of work that you can perform as you continue to age, possibly with less physical stamina. If you're a cowboy who lassos and brands steers, it's time to keep your eyes open for a desk job back at the ranch.

How much money should you save up and earmark for retirement? While the future returns of the market are unknown, we think that if you're 50 years old, your retirement at age 70 is on its way to being fully self-funded if you presently have about four times your current household income in a tax-deferred retirement account, provided that you continue to save.

If you're 55, your retirement is on its way to being fully funded if you have about six times your household's income in that same account. If you have less than this saved up by this point (undoubtedly the case for most people), then you probably need to be socking away a significantly greater portion of your income every year to prepare for that time when you no longer want to—or can—work. See Table 17.1 for a suggested amount.

169

Table 17.1: Optimized Savings Rates as % of Current Salary for Constant Pre- & Post-Retirement Standard of Living		
If You Have in Savings:	**You Should Save:**	
	Age 50	**Age 55**
No Retirement Savings	35%	44%
Savings = 1 Year's Salary	30%	39%
Savings = 2 Years' Salary	26%	34%
Savings = 3 Years' Salary	17%	29%
Savings = 4 Years' Salary	8%	24%
Savings = 5 Years' Salary	0%	19%
Savings = 6 Years' Salary	0%	8%
Savings = 7 Years' Salary	0%	0%

If the recommended savings amount is over 16 percent of your pretax salary, we're no longer assuming that you'll be retiring on the ideal of 84 percent of your preretirement income. Rather, we've simply tried to optimize the savings so that your standard of living can be as high as possible going forward from today, with no perceived bump when you actually stop working.

Meanwhile, Table 17.2 shows how much you ideally should have accumulated in your retirement accounts by now (assuming that you'll keep saving going forward).

Table 17.2: Are Your Retirement Savings on Track? Multiple of Current Salary You Should Have in Savings	
Age	**Retirement Savings**
50	4
55	6
60	9

At this point, for those without savings, it cruelly becomes a simple issue of saving every penny possible while postponing retirement indefinitely. A reminder: These tables assume that you won't be getting a penny from Social Security or any pension plan, so you'll have to pay for your entire retirement yourself. If you anticipate income from these sources, you'll need far less in the way of supplementary savings.

Remember that if you "ESPlanned" the smoothing of your lifetime consumption by diverting dollars that were formerly going toward your retirement account into the purchase of your home and your children's education, most of those scenarios called for you to resume saving with a vengeance once that last tuition check was in the mail. Don't assume that the money you now have left over is just extra income available for spending on a trip to Hong Kong, however much you may feel that you deserve it.

You're getting close enough to retirement that you should do the kind of detailed calculation that your authors proposed in their previous work *Yes, You Can Still Retire Comfortably!* For even more detail, you could buy your own copy of ESPlanner and see whether the golf course at Millionaire Acres lies in your future. Just keep in mind that all models are only as good as the assumptions underlying them. These provide the best answers we know of, but living is dangerous and there are no guarantees. This is why there's a strong argument for overpreparing.

Once you're ten years away from your retirement date (which you may decide to make earlier than we recommend—you pick the date), here's a method to get a fix on your savings needs:

Step 1: Multiply your current household income by 0.84. We're going to assume that you can live on 84 percent of your current income (again, adjusted for no longer adding to savings) after you retire, on average. Admittedly, this figure is controversial. If you want a better number, go through your expenditures for the past year (more easily done if you routinely use Quicken or Money) and sort out how they are likely to change after you stop working. But don't forget those huge expenses such as cars and new roofs that you'll undoubtedly need, but which may not have shown up in last year's budget.

Inevitably you'll also be picking up a bigger piece of your medical-care expenses as the government finds various ways to ratchet back its promised subsidy. Over time, this adjustment could have a huge impact on your capital requirements all by itself. On the other hand, you'll no longer be salting away money with FICA or in your retirement savings accounts every year.

Step 2: Deduct from the dollar amount you calculated in Step 1 whatever income you think you'll be getting from Social Security or from your defined benefit pension plan, if any (assuming that yours will be solvent). Be conservative here, because your defined benefit pension plan probably isn't indexed for inflation (or is it . . . you'd better find out), which could easily cut its spending power in half in 20 years. For anyone rich enough to afford this book, Social Security will probably be given a buzz cut as well.

Now you have an estimate of how much income you'll need to replace every year to maintain your standard of living once retired.

Step 3: Most studies suggest that 4 percent is a safe annual withdrawal rate, in which case you need to have 25 times the above amount (determined in Step 2) in your nest egg when you retire. Again, this is probably a worst-case scenario. A 6 percent withdrawal rate would require a nest egg of only about 17 times this amount on the day you retire. It's likely that this will be doable in many possible economic futures—but not if you retire on the day the next Great Depression begins. If you build a nest egg that's 20 times your annual draw, you'll be that much more secure.

Step 4: Divide the total that you currently have in dedicated retirement savings by the amount of this nest egg; the result will be some percentage. If you have $500,000 in your retirement accounts, and you need $1 million for your final nest egg to maintain your living standard, then you currently have 50 percent of what you need.

Step 5: Consult Table 17.3.

**Table 17.3: Percentage of Nest Egg to Save Annually
for People Starting 10 Years from Retirement**

If You Have in Savings:	You Should Save:	
(Savings as % of Nest Egg)	Median Investment Returns	Low Investment Returns
0%	6.3%	7.0%
5%	5.7%	6.5%
10%	5.1%	5.9%
15%	4.5%	5.4%
20%	3.9%	4.8%
25%	3.3%	4.3%
30%	2.7%	3.8%
35%	2.1%	3.3%
40%	1.5%	2.8%
45%	0.9%	2.2%
50%	0.3%	1.7%
55%	0.0%	1.1%
60%	0.0%	0.6%
65%	0.0%	0.0%

Go down the left-hand column of Table 17.3 until you find the number that matches the percentage of income you already have saved up (which you determined in Step 4). Then go across to the appropriate figure. You can use the "Median" column if you believe that investment returns going forward will resemble those in the past. You can go with the "20%ile" (20th percentile) in the next column if you believe that investment returns will be significantly lower over the next decade than in the past, or if you want to save with a higher margin of safety. Either way, this will give you the magic multiplier.

Step 6: Multiply this magic percentage by the total dollar amount of the nest egg that you'll need (as you calculated in Step 3). The product of this equation is the number of dollars that you need to invest each and every year for the next ten years in order to grow that nest egg. You should augment this amount by the rate of inflation every year.

For example, let's say that you determine that ten years hence, you'll need a nest egg of $1 million. Then you look in your retirement accounts and find that they're worth $450,000 as of today, or 45 percent of the total nest egg you'll need.

You go to Table 17.3 and discover that this corresponds to a multiplier of 0.90 percent of the total nest egg that you need to save every year. If the total next egg is $1 million, then 0.90 percent times $1 million gives you a recommended annual savings of $9,000 per year for the next decade, adjusting this amount annually by inflation.

If the market returns going forward are what they have been in the past, this should get you there. If you want to be more sure of hitting your mark, you might decide to only bank on getting the 20th percentile of investment returns going forward, and so save an inflation-adjusted $22,000 yearly for the next decade.

Note that this assumes that the money is going to be invested in tax-deferred accounts. If it's going into a taxable account, we're assuming that you're paying any capital gains and dividend taxes out of your own pocket, not out of the accumulating funds. Because we suspect that the bulk of these monies will be in 401(k) plans, we've also assumed that the total expense ratios are under one percent annually.

Investing

Once you get within ten years of retirement, we propose that you take a walk on the tame side with your asset allocation. You no longer have the luxury of time or increased earnings to power you through any sudden hit in the market. We want your portfolio to look like Figure 17.2.

Figure 17.2: Asset Allocation Approaching Retirement

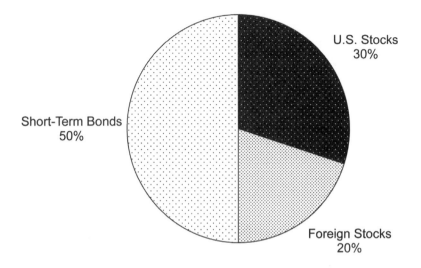

U.S. Stocks
30%

Short-Term Bonds
50%

Foreign Stocks
20%

We've made the allocation safer by decreasing the stocks from **175** 60 to 50 percent. Please don't fail to move your portfolio in a conservative direction as you approach the day when you'll quit working. Many a retirement plan has hit the rocks when people assumed that they had plenty of money in the bank, failed to sufficiently protect their assets, and then the market took a cruel turn. Unfortunately, this happens all the time.

Old Folks in Homes

Growing old isn't for the faint of heart. You're probably plenty sick of hearing about preparing for retirement. While it's the main money problem of the 50s, there are others. More than half of all seniors will one day require long-term care in a nursing home, which presently clocks in at about $75,000 a year (with an average stay being two and one-half years). Meanwhile, Congress has just made sure that you can no longer give away your assets to your children in order to qualify for a Medicaid-covered stay.

Hence the need for long-term-care insurance. The problem is that these policies are extremely expensive, and a number of the ones that have been sold thus far are of questionable worth. If you're poor, you can't afford them, which is fine, because you'll qualify for Medicaid in any event. If you're rich, you can afford to self-insure, so you don't need this product either. But if you're in the middle class, you're in a pickle. At some point in your 50s or 60s, you should probably buy one of these policies if you can possibly afford it.

Long-term-care insurance policies are the study of a lifetime, so be sure to do a lot of research before buying one. Look them up in *Consumer Reports* and any other guide you can find (the Stein-DeMuth Website links to a useful one from Weiss Ratings), because the pitfalls are too numerous to detail here.

But wait—there's more. Everyone has parents, and they're aging every day. When dear old Mom and Pop get old, they often become weak and infirm, and sometimes that means that they have to go into a nursing home. This is sad, but it happens.

If you've ever seen nursing homes, you know that some of them are lovely, charming places—and some of them are snake pits. It's no secret that those with higher costs tend to be the lovelier places, while the ones paid for by Medicaid tend to offer depressing, miserable care. It's bad enough to be old, but to also be in a dark, noisy, unclean atmosphere with thug-like attendants is truly horrible. If your parents have to go into a nursing home, you don't want them feeling that they've been led to the gulag.

For many boomers, this means that their folks may have to rely on the kiddies—who are now probably in their 50s or older—to pick up the tab. To be perfectly blunt about it, paying for that stay at Golden Palms can cost you a fortune. If you feel that it's your duty to pick up the nursing-home tab for Mom and Dad, you'd better make some provision for those huge monthly bills. You might want to have a word with your spouse about it as well, since this can quickly break a family's budget.

Many boomers are now facing the perfect storm:

- They delayed having kids, so they're in their 50s with their children's expensive educations still to pay for.

- They've underfunded their own retirement plans, so they're woefully behind the eight ball in that department.

- And now they also have aging parents who are headed for the nursing home or otherwise require substantial transfusions of cash and personal care just to keep them afloat.

This is real financial misery. You can prepare for the possible cost of your parents' care either by paying for it as you go or by setting aside some kind of reserve. Or, better still, you can insure against this situation by helping your parents buy the insurance for themselves.

How (and whether) you choose to make such preparations is up to you, but this is a thunderstorm that breaks into a great many lives. If Mom or Dad does need help, you can expect that it won't be cheap.

There's Good News?

Despite all this grim talk, there are some good financial tidings. In most cases, if you're part of a family, you'll be well on your way to owning your home. You'll probably have seen its worth increase significantly, while inflation has eaten away the cost of the monthly payment. It's likely that your other investments have also increased substantially in value. Not only that, but on the consumption side, your days of big surprises are probably over—except for parental care, as just discussed. Your house is presumably furnished more or less the way you like it, and your chances of getting divorced in your 50s are only a fraction of what they were when you were in your late 20s or early 30s.

If you're on the road to providing adequately for your retirement, and if you aren't caught by surprise if Mom or Dad has to go to Golden Palms Nursing Home, then anything that you earn above your basic expenses now is gravy.

◢ ◥ ◢

CHAPTER 18

In Your 60s
and Beyond

There's only one major financial event for most persons in their 60s and older, and that's retirement. For the remaining years on the job, income typically is flat to falling as you work fewer hours or take on less challenging assignments. Figure 18.1 shows what remains of the income curve for people who continue to work full-time throughout the year.

**Figure 18.1: Inflation-Adjusted Income
in Your 60s and Beyond**

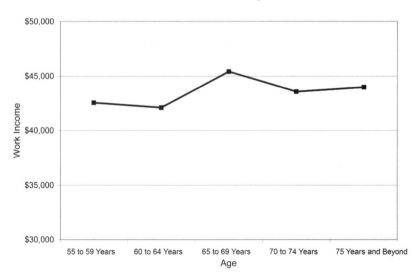

Of course, your earned income generally falls off a cliff when you retire. Without proper preparation, this will be the most sudden and devastating financial shock of your life. For many people, there will be no way to stretch their meager savings across the chasm that looms ahead. What are their options?

Don't Retire

The best choice for most people who are unprepared is simply to postpone retirement. Fortunately for baby boomers, jobs will likely be plentiful, given the shortage of workers in the generations that follow. This self-created (through having fewer children) labor shortage means that there should be better-paying and more interesting jobs available than just being Wal-Mart greeters.

It may be that the entire model of retirement we've inherited—knocking a golf ball around the course for 20 or 30 years, followed by extensive cocktailing—is overrated. Having more leisure time than you can constructively handle is more of a curse than a blessing. Work is the ultimate antidepressant, antipsychotic, and antianxiety agent.

The money in your pocket won't hurt your disposition any, either. By putting off retirement, you allow your nest egg to be disbursed over fewer years, thereby boosting your standard of living. It also lets you postpone taking Social Security, which will increase your payout there as well when you finally pull the trigger.

Relocation

The second best way to make your dollars go further is by selling your house and relocating to an area with a lower cost of living. We're all familiar with the concept of the empty nest. You and your spouse bought a split-level ranch house in Smallville years ago when Junior and Sis needed more privacy. Now you're contemplating leaving your home and moving to Eden Isle, Arkansas. Imagine that you bought your house in 1983 for $100,000; today, it could be sold for $500,000.

180

But wait a minute: You've paid off the mortgage, so it's free to live there, right? Wrong. The true cost of that house to you is how much interest you could be earning were the proceeds from selling it, properly invested. If you put your house's value in an account at 6 percent interest, you'll earn $30,000 each year, just from the interest—so it's effectively costing you that much every year to keep it.

(Actually, you won't get quite that much, because you'll incur transaction costs in unlocking this value in the form of a real-estate commission in selling the house, plus other expenses attendant upon relocating. These could add up to as much as 10 percent, so you might use $27,000 as a more realistic figure.)

You may find a condo to die for in Eden Isle for $250,000, which would cost you about half of what you're now paying each month. And don't forget that the cost of living is significantly cheaper there. You could buy the condo outright and invest the remaining money, using the interest to buy golf balls and airplane tickets. In other words, you might be able to add greatly to your financial assets by selling that old "free" house.

The retiree or potential retiree would do well to find out just how much the old homestead is worth (try **www.zillow.com** for a first take; the Stein-DeMuth Website also has some useful links regarding the relocation process). If the forgone interest implicit in owning your current house is a lot more than the cost of new digs, maybe you ought to call your Realtor and see what you can do. A valuable house with no mortgage payment and virtually no taxes can still cost a fortune from month to month because of the forgone interest. The retiree who may have difficultly making ends meet can sell and relocate to a cheaper part of the country and take a big step toward a more secure way of life in the process.

One note of caution: Should you find that you own a home in an area that's rising rapidly in value, you should hold on to it. The growth in value likely outstrips any yield that you could get with the proceeds from selling. Of course, you'll rarely run into this situation unless your house happens to be in Manhattan or Laguna Beach.

The next two solutions to the retiree's money worries should only be undertaken after a thorough analysis of his or her financial situation—preferably after a one-time consultation with an

181

YES, YOU CAN GET A FINANCIAL LIFE!

impartial, fee-based financial planner who doesn't want to sell you anything and has no stake in the outcome.

Immediate Annuities

Your authors have written about the benefits of immediate annuities at length in *Yes, You Can Still Retire Comfortably!*, so there's no need to repeat ourselves here. These products allow you to convert a pile of savings into the largest possible payout, distributed over your lifetime. Vanguard (and others) even offers a fixed annuity that's indexed to inflation.

Otherwise, you'll want to consider having some combination of fixed and variable annuities. The latter tie your payout to a portfolio of stocks and/or bonds, allowing it to increase over time and thus keep up with mild inflation (with the risk being that the payout can decrease if the markets head south).

The downside is that fees still tend to be high, and the contract provisions can be bewilderingly complicated. Once the papers are signed, the decision to annuitize is practically irreversible—getting out of them is sort of like trying to get your money back from a Las Vegas casino after your roulette number doesn't come up. Don't sign anything until you've read and understood every word of the contract. (There's a market in this, by the way.) But from the consumer's point of view, the annuities are changing in ways that are all to the good: The trend is toward increasing transparency, simplified contracts, lower fees, and easier withdrawal should you change your mind.

Reverse Mortgages

If you know that you'll love living in your house until the day you die, a reverse mortgage is another option. The basic idea is to use your home as collateral for a loan, which is only repaid from the sale of your residence after you move out. Again, let us refer you to our more extensive discussion of these products in *Yes, You*

Can Still Retire Comfortably! rather than just repeat ourselves. Our Website (**www.stein-demuth.com**) can link you to some other sites (such as AARP, Financial Freedom, and HUD) that you'll find extremely helpful if you want to investigate reverse mortgages.

Note that these can be combined with relocation to a cheaper area of the country: You can buy your home in Eden Isle, Arkansas, outright and immediately take out a reverse mortgage against it. (Actually, Eden Isle has become quite expensive, although not compared with Manhattan.)

As with immediate annuities, there are serious consequences for your estate with reverse mortgages. This isn't a contract to be rushed into without a lot of due diligence on your part. Inevitably, the question will be whether the trade-offs are worth it in your situation.

1,000 Natural Shocks

The human body wears out. This has religious and moral importance, and it also has financial significance. Sometimes a person may have to go to the hospital for a very long period. This is known as catastrophic illness, and unfortunately for those 65 or older, it happens about ten times as often as it does to those who are only 35. When you're older, all your sins of diet and lifestyle (plus some new ones) catch up with you, along with heredity, and it can cost you a lot of money. Lengthy stays in the hospital are expensive on a scale once contemplated only by timber barons.

For the present, Medicare pays for 20 days of nursing-home care at full coverage and 80 days at partial coverage. Then it stops. Many situations aren't covered at all. What's more, it's scarcely written in granite that these benefits will remain as generous as they are today.

According to the programs' trustees, the long-term liabilities of Social Security and Medicare are $65.9 trillion. This amount is greater than the total wealth of the United States. This means as a nation, we are technically bankrupt right now. The total wealth of the nation is about half that amount. As economist Herbert Stein

183

(Ben's dad) famously said, "If something cannot go on forever, it will stop." In its present form, America's senior-entitlement program is one of those trends that's going to stop, unfortunately for the people involved (who happen to be us).

As we've seen with the latest round of proposed Social Security reforms, this is a can of worms that the government keeps kicking down the road, and there's no reason to believe that anything meaningful will be done until some major crisis hits—by which time the problem will be of such glaring magnitude that the government solution will possibly be to socialize the entire health-care economy and severely ration treatment.

Under this scenario, if you need medical attention and you're poor or middle class, you'll stand in line and hope that you don't die waiting. If you're rich, you'll be treated immediately, but at a high price that you'll pay yourself.

As an older American, you should have some kind of health program that will cover you in the event of catastrophic illness. At a minimum, you're going to need a Medicare supplement ("Medigap") policy. Ideally, you should have a long-term-care insurance policy as well, unless, again, you're so rich that you can self-insure or so poor that you don't need one. The day may come when you wish you had a large chunk of private savings to bypass the waiting lists and buy the health care you need wherever it's still available.

Remember Inflation?

During the late '60s and early '70s, the United States went through the worst peacetime inflation (and the longest such phenomenon during either war or peace) in our nation's history. The average market basket of goods and services that cost $100 in 1967 was up to more than $300 by 1980.

Inflation has a nasty habit of coming back when you least expect it, sort of like a summer cold. For working people, those sudden flare-ups can be bad enough. However, at least they can try to get their wages adjusted or raise their fees. The retired person who's no longer in the labor force has a far more serious problem.

Even "benign" inflation is anathema to anyone living on a fixed income. At a modest 3.6 percent rate, the value of a dollar is cut in half in 20 years—well within a retiree's projected life span. In other words, without an inflation adjustment, a $50,000 income stream at age 65 is going to spend like $25,000 when you're 85, under ordinary assumptions. And yet, at age 85, you may not feel like going back to work to earn the money necessary to keep your electricity turned on.

In one way, this declining purchasing power is in accord with retirees' spending habits. People tend to be more active in early retirement and more quiescent (thus spending less) later on. The problem is that those later years are when the really big health-care crises hit. Boomers may have the unpleasant prospect of facing catastrophic medical bills at precisely the time when their few dollars that remain are worth far less, and the government programs that were supposed to save them are bankrupt. Ouch! This is another perfect storm heading our way.

There are ways to hedge inflation. Real estate such as your home typically appreciates in tandem with inflation. You can buy a diversified basket of real estate investment trusts in a mutual fund, such as Vanguard's Real Estate Viper (ticker VNQ), for example, or Cohen & Steers Realty Majors (ticker ICF).

185

Commodities like soy beans and pork bellies also are closely tied to inflation. You're unlikely to buy these directly, but again, you can invest in a diversified basket of commodities in a mutual fund such as the Goldman Sachs Natural Resources Index (ticker IGE), for another example.

Finally, you can purchase U.S. government bonds that pay a low yield, but one whose principal is stepped up in line with the consumer price index. These Treasury Inflation-Protected Securities can be bought directly from the government, or you can buy a mutual fund that invests in a pool of them, such as the iShares Treasury Inflation-Protected Securities Fund (ticker TIP).

Assets like these will hedge against a sudden spike in inflation that would be extremely disruptive to the bond and stock markets. For dealing with more prolonged, "benign" inflation, your best defense is to continue to invest in the stock market throughout your retirement, or in some investment product that is pegged to the market, such as a variable annuity. In other words, don't just move all your money into tax-free municipal bonds on the day you retire and assume that the yield they're currently giving will provide for you for the rest of your life. This is yet another good reason to look into variable annuities as well.

Investing in Retirement

Once you've left your employer, it will almost certainly be to your advantage to roll over your 401(k) into an IRA at a low-expense custodian such as Vanguard or Fidelity, where you'll have better and cheaper investment options.

The next change we recommend is diversifying your bond portfolio into Treasury Inflation-Protected Securities, assuming that you can keep these in a tax-deferred account (where you won't have to pay taxes on any phantom income these securities throw off). If you can't do this for whatever reason, don't worry about it—short-term bonds (or even intermediate ones, such as a fund that tracks the Lehman Brothers Aggregate Bond Index) should be fine. On the equity side, ideally your U.S. stocks include some exposure to small cap stocks (such as total stock market funds provide), and your foreign stock funds provide exposure to emerging markets, as well as the Morgan Stanley EAFE Index. Your base retirement allocation should look like Figure 18.2.

186

Figure 18.2: Retirement Asset Allocation

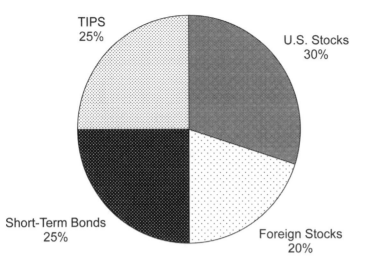

TIPS
25%

U.S. Stocks
30%

Short-Term Bonds
25%

Foreign Stocks
20%

This is as fancy as you need to get with your retirement investing. However, if you want to further diversify your portfolio, you might want to consider investing a portion of your assets directly in various kinds of income-producing securities. Conveniently, your authors have written a book on the subject *(Yes, You Can Be a Successful Income Investor!)* that we recommend consulting if you want to move in this direction. You'll find a link to it from our Website.

187

In general, it's also better to keep bonds and TIPS in tax-deferred accounts because their coupons are taxable as ordinary income, while the dividends and long-term capital gains from equities are usually subject to the friendly rate of 15 percent in taxable accounts. Of course, if the Bush tax cuts are allowed to expire, then all bets are off. If there isn't enough headroom to keep all your bonds in your tax-deferred account, then you can always switch to municipal bonds and hold them in your taxable account as an alternative. Your best course of action here will depend on your tax bracket in retirement.

Drawing Down

Since you will be periodically (perhaps every quarter) drawing upon your nest egg to raise money for living expenses, we recommend taking the money from whatever piece of the above portfolio pie has performed the best lately. In this way, you'll be continually rebalancing your portfolio by selling whichever asset has had the greatest price appreciation (also known as "selling high").

It's generally advised to take the money from your taxable accounts first, since this preserves the advantage of tax-deferred compounding for your IRA, Keogh, and 401(k) accounts for as long as possible. But if you follow this approach, don't drain your stocks in your taxable accounts down to zero while leaving nothing but bonds in your tax-deferred accounts to withdraw later. Try to keep the overall allocation as shown in Figure 18.1., even if this means that you have to start buying stocks in the tax-deferred accounts to keep your allocation in overall balance.

How much can you afford to withdraw? This question has been debated by all the deepest thinkers, with no definitive answer. We've recently been impressed with the Quantext Portfolio Planner developed by former NASA scientist Geoff Considine, and currently available for a free trial at **www.quantext.com**. We plugged the portfolio above into this Monte Carlo simulator (think of it as a flight simulator for portfolios instead of planes) and experimented with different draw-down rates. Given that the future is unknowable, it's impossible to fine-tune withdrawal rates to perfection, but we wanted to provide an intelligent estimate.

The first year, we calculated our income by multiplying the total nest egg by an initial withdrawal rate. For example, a $1 million nest egg multiplied by a 5 percent withdrawal rate would result in a $50,000 cash withdrawal. Then every year after that, we'd take out this same dollar amount, only adjusted each time for inflation. If it were 3 percent during the first year, then the second year we'd take out $50,000 plus 3 percent of that amount ($1,500), for a total withdrawal during year two of $51,500 . . . and so on for every year thereafter. You'll find a link to the current inflation rate on the Stein-DeMuth Website.

In terms of calculating the safety of a given rate of withdrawal, we used the Quantext Portfolio Planner to calculate how many years the nest egg could support us at each initial withdrawal rate before encountering a 10 percent chance of running out of money. Or, to put it differently, we measured how many years we might merrily go along with various initial withdrawal rates, with a 90 percent assurance that our portfolios would remain solvent. The results are shown in Figure 18.3.

Figure 18.3: Nest Egg Initial Withdrawal Rates

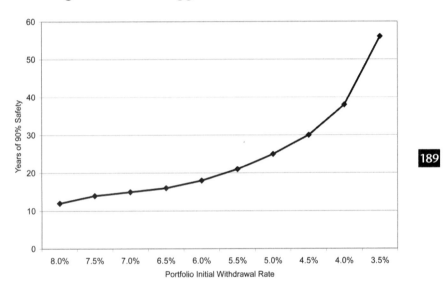

The main finding that jumps off the page is that the greater your withdrawal rate, the fewer years you can pull from your portfolio with a high margin of safety. Start with 8 percent and continue to withdraw this dollar amount every year, adjusting for inflation along the way, and you only have about 12 years of relative assurance that your portfolio will support you. Of course, the stock market may take off like a rocket, and you'll do fine. But here we're focusing on the other end of the scale: The chance of earning low returns coupled with a high withdrawal might lead to an early financial demise. The "bad-case" analysis is relevant to retirees, because they typically don't have the ability to go out and earn a lot of new money if bad times hit.

At the other end of the spectrum, if you only pull 3.5 percent from your savings, they might support you for 56 years before you run into trouble—a long retirement by anyone's standard. Even so, these withdrawal rates are a bit lower than those suggested in *Yes, You Can Still Retire Comfortably!* because they're more sensitive to the lower returns that the stock and bond markets have been delivering of late (which are expected to continue, going forward from today's elevated market valuation levels).

You can eyeball your savings, estimate the length of your retirement based on your age and projected longevity, and then come up with an initial withdrawal rate that makes sense in your situation.

A corollary from Figure 18.3 is that *the further you get into retirement, the more you might be able to safely dip into your nest egg.* If you retired at 65 taking out $50,000 a year from a $1 million nest egg, you're now 85 years old, and your nest egg is still doing well thanks to the beneficence of the stock market, you might want to recalculate your retirement withdrawals based on a higher rate. Realistically, your portfolio now only has to shepherd you over a shorter period of time. For the same reason, you can also shift to a more aggressive asset allocation in late retirement, such as that shown in figure 18.4.

Figure 18.4: Late Retirement Asset Allocation

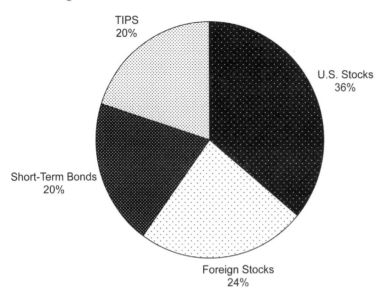

TIPS
20%

U.S. Stocks
36%

Short-Term Bonds
20%

Foreign Stocks
24%

191

Estate Planning

How much should you bequeath to your children? We all want our heirs to have a happier, easier life than we did, and we want to be remembered and appreciated. We hope that we can make these good things happen by leaving money to our kids. This leads many retirees, even those who are hard up for cash, to refuse to dig into any more of their savings than necessary for survival, so as to not despoil the sums they hope to leave to the next generation.

Economists, on the other hand, believe that the real contribution that most parents make is to leave behind a generally wealthier and more prosperous world. Consider how much easier our lives have been than those of previous generations of Americans. For example, lower-class people today live better than the middle class did only 50 years ago. Economists have also noted that if your bequest is like all too many, it will quickly be spent on trifles, leaving your heirs with a distorted sense of values about money, undoing their work habits, and making them less (rather than more) self-reliant.

Of course, your gifts can also do a great deal of good. Our point is only that in the last financial passage of your earthly stay, you may well be faced with some hard decisions regarding your own expenditures. In making those choices, you may well weigh just how much or how little you want to leave to your children. If you decide to spend more on yourself, providing for your own well-being and leaving your children to do the same for themselves, you aren't making a cruel or unusual choice.

Obviously, if you're a conduit through which a large hereditary fortune has passed, your decision should differ from that of an ordinary working man or woman. But for most people, the option of improving their own financial security after retirement by reducing their likely bequests is widely used.

Your first responsibility is to take care of yourself. When we do for others, expecting their care in return, we're usually asking for trouble (reread *King Lear* for more on this). You can make your life less heartbreaking if you simply emphasize self-care from the outset. The final financial task of your retirement years is to leave things in good order for those who will survive you, which means having a will, and very possibly putting your assets into some sort of trust. This should be drawn up by an attorney who specializes in estate planning, not written on the back of a napkin while you're in the hospital awaiting surgery. Speaking of which, you'll also want to give someone power of attorney so that they can make medical decisions on your behalf.

Once your estate plan is in place, it's an excellent idea to leave a letter for the trustee of your estate that shares such useful tidbits as the locations of:

- Your will
- Paper statements for all your accounts
- Tax forms
- Insurance policies
- Safe-deposit box(es)
- Keys for the safe-deposit box(es)
- Online account numbers, IDs, and passwords

Also include the names and contact information for your:

- Attorney

- Tax preparer

- Investment advisor

- Any funeral arrangements you've made

- Anyone else officially involved in your legal and financial affairs

In other words, this is a "kitchen-sink" document that includes everything you'd want to have, were you in your trustee's shoes. If you can postpone dying for a bit, your authors are writing just such a workbook to help you get all this organized.

We'll close by offering you a sensational idea that will more than repay you for the time spent reading our book: We recommend that your estate bequests also include individual letters written to each of those people closest to you, telling them how much you love them and what they've meant to you. Let your children know how proud you are of them. In the letters, write down everything you ever wanted to tell them but perhaps felt too awkward to say face-to-face. We all go through life making sacrifices every day, often starved for even the most minimal appreciation or acknowledgment for our efforts. Your letter will be like a love bomb that will explode in their hearts and be remembered forever.

193

▰ ◤ ▰

CONCLUSION

Wₑ're all only flesh and blood. We make terrible mistakes, have great hopes that are destroyed, and routinely invite totally unnecessary suffering into our lives. On the other hand, we have the possibility of enjoying a measure of happiness and contentment as well.

Sadly, much sorrow and anxiety comes from mistakes in handling money. This book is an attempt to make your life happier by pointing out the potholes and canceled flights on life's journey, and then suggesting how to work around them. You don't take any money with you when you leave, but you can at least try to be a good steward of what life (we'd say, God) has given you before you shuffle off this mortal coil.

Here are ten commandments for coping with life's predictable financial crises, a brief summary of what you should remember to claim your financial life:

1. Your first goal should be to increase your human capital by getting a solid education and developing excellent work habits, making connections, and cultivating a pleasant personality.

2. Start saving for retirement as early as possible. Set up an IRA or 401(k) and fund it aggressively, starting as soon as you hit the job market. Once this is in place, put some

additional money aside until you have a modest reserve fund built up for emergencies.

3. Your next savings goal should be for the down payment on a house and raising the children you'll likely have one day. If you can start to save for five years before you move ahead with these life changes, it will go a long way toward smoothing out your lifestyle.

4. Get—and stay—married to a sensible person.

5. Don't show off by buying expensive, high-status possessions or consuming leisure in a way that projects a lifestyle you can't afford.

6. Work full-time, year-round, and acquire seniority; don't hopscotch from one unrelated job to another unless you're jumping a step up. If at all possible, raise your own personal productivity by keeping yourself well educated, well informed, and well connected in your line of work. Remember that almost everything good that happens in life is the result of personal contacts.

7. Don't make any financial moves that will either contribute to the likelihood of a divorce or make life unbearably hard if such an event were to occur. Don't make major financial decisions in a marriage unilaterally—you and your spouse both need to "buy into" your plans together.

8. Make your children pay for their own college education to the extent that it's possible and necessary. They're acquiring a capital asset, and they should pay for it.

9. Don't expect that you have the right to live luxuriously as you enter middle age and beyond. People can afford to live as well as their finances allow—not as well as they feel entitled to live.

10. Don't swing for the fences with your investments. Risk and reward are joined at the hip. Use low-expense index funds to broadly diversify your holdings so that you get returns commensurate with the amount of risk you're taking. Then stay invested through thick and thin.

◼◥◼

Index

ABOUT THE AUTHORS

Greg Bertolini

Ben Stein can be seen talking about finance on Fox TV news every week and writing about it regularly in *The New York Times* Sunday Business Section. No wonder: Not only is he the son of the world-famous economist and government advisor Herbert Stein, but Ben is a respected economist in his own right. He received his B.A. with honors in economics from Columbia University in 1966, studied economics in the graduate school of economics at Yale while he earned his law degree there, and worked as an economist for the Department of Commerce.

Ben Stein is known to many as a movie and television personality, especially from *Ferris Bueller's Day Off* and from his long-running quiz show, *Win Ben Stein's Money*. But he has probably worked more in personal and corporate finance than anything else.

He has written about finance for *Barron's* and *The Wall Street Journal* for decades. He was one of the chief busters of the junk-bond frauds of the 1980s, has been a long-time critic of corporate executives' self-dealing, and has written three self-help books about personal finance. He frequently travels the country speaking about finance in both serious and humorous ways. He is the honorary chair of the National Retirement Planning Coalition.

Website: **www.benstein.com**

Greg Bertolini

Phil DeMuth was the valedictorian of his class at the University of California at Santa Barbara in 1972, then took his master's in communications and Ph.D. in clinical psychology. Both a psychologist and registered investment advisor, Phil has written for *The Wall Street Journal*, *Barron's*, the *Louis Rukeyser Newsletter*, the *Journal of Financial Planning*, and **forbes.com**, as well as *Human Behavior* and *Psychology Today.* His opinions have been quoted in **theStreet.com**, *Yahoo! Finance, On Wall Street*, and *Fortune* magazine, and he has been profiled in *Research* magazine and seen on *Forbes on Fox* and *Wall Street Week.* He is Managing Director of Conservative Wealth Management LLC in Los Angeles, a registered investment advisor to high-net-worth individuals, institutions, and foundations.

Website: **www.phildemuth.com**

NOTES

NOTES

NOTES

Notes

NOTES

NOTES

NOTES

Notes

NBP

We hope you enjoyed this book.
If you'd like additional information, please contact
New Beginnings Press through their distributors:

Hay House, Inc.
P.O. Box 5100
Carlsbad, CA 92018-5100

(760) 431-7695 or (800) 654-5126
(760) 431-6948 (fax) or (800) 650-5115 (fax)
www.hayhouse.com® • www.hayfoundation.org

Distributed in Australia by: Hay House Australia
Pty. Ltd., 18/36 Ralph St., Alexandria NSW 2015 • *Phone:* 612-9669-4299
Fax: 612-9669-4144 • www.hayhouse.com.au

Distributed in the United Kingdom by: Hay House UK, Ltd.,
292B Kensal Rd., London W10 5BE • *Phone:* 44-20-8962-1230
Fax: 44-20-8962-1239 • www.hayhouse.co.uk

Distributed in the Republic of South Africa by:
Hay House SA (Pty), Ltd., P.O. Box 990, Witkoppen 2068
Phone/Fax: 27-11-706-6612 • orders@psdprom.co.za

Distributed in India by: Hay House Publications (India) Pvt. Ltd.,
Muskaan Complex, Plot No. 3, B-2, Vasant Kunj, New Delhi 110 070
Phone: 91-11-4176-1620 • *Fax:* 91-11-4176-1630
www.hayhouseindia.co.in

Distributed in Canada by: Raincoast, 9050 Shaughnessy St.,
Vancouver, B.C. V6P 6E5 • *Phone:* (604) 323-7100
Fax: (604) 323-2600 • www.raincoast.com

Tune in to **HayHouseRadio.com®** for the best in inspirational
talk radio featuring top Hay House authors! And, sign up via the
Hay House USA Website to receive the Hay House online newsletter
and stay informed about what's going on with your favorite authors.
You'll receive bimonthly announcements about: Discounts and Offers,
Special Events, Product Highlights, Free Excerpts, Giveaways, and more!
www.hayhouse.com®